WHY WE'RE HERE

The Powerful Impact of Public Broadcasters
When They *Turn Outward*

Richard C. Harwood & Aaron B. Leavy

For information about permission to reproduce selections from this book, write to:
    Permissions
    Kettering Foundation Press
    200 Commons Road
    Dayton, Ohio 45459

First Edition, 2011
Manufactured in the United States of America
Design by Justin Kemerling
Library of Congress Cataloging-in-Publication-Data

    Why We're Here: The Powerful Impact of Public Broadcasters
    When They Turn Outward
    p. cm
    ISBN 978-0-923993-33-7

*For Emily and Jonathan—who always
remind me of why I'm here.*

RCH

*For my parents, who endured and
embraced my compulsion to ask
the next question. And from whom
I received both roots and wings.*

ABL

TABLE OF CONTENTS

WHY WE'RE HERE

PREFACE

THIS BOOK IS PRIMARILY about public broadcasters and their relationship to community and public life. But this book could be about any organization or group that seeks to be actively engaged in communities.

Over the past 20 years, the Harwood Institute has been creating alliances and partnerships with organizations that want their efforts to be more relevant and significant in the life of communities. These groups recognize that their own path forward requires them to innovate and be more intentional in relating to communities, engaging and mobilizing people, forging new networks, and generating a positive impact in people's lives.

None of this change comes easily—nothing good ever does. But over the years, we've discovered that such change is within reach of individuals and organizations that are willing to turn outward toward their communities and become more intentional in the judgments and choices they make in seeking genuine impact.

As this book goes to press we are in the midst of another major partnership, this time with United Way Worldwide (uww), in which the ideas and approaches found here will be diffused throughout the United Way system which includes nearly 1,800 member organizations across the world. Moreover, we are also forging such alliances with another handful of nationally networked organizations to help change the DNA of how they relate to and work in communities.

The institute's vision is that in communities across the United States, there will be new emerging hubs of public broadcasters, local United Ways, and thousands of other individuals and organizations who have made our ideas and approaches their own and are starting to work together, support one another, and ultimately create a different kind of public life. We see this happening already. Our commitment is to help create a new force for change in public life that is rooted in communities and focused on generating impact in people's lives—and which helps restore our confidence and belief in one another and our collective ability to take effective civic action.

So as you read about the efforts of public broadcasters, and admire their good work, think also about the organizations and individuals you know—including yourself—and their potential to step forward, innovate, and bring greater intentionality to their efforts to create hope and change in communities and public life in America.

It all starts with a turn outward.

WHY WE'RE HERE

D URING A RECENT CONVERSATION, our good friend Joe Krushinsky, Vice President for Institutional Advancement from Maryland Public Television, unknowingly gave us the title of this book, and we are grateful to him. When talking about the essence of public broadcasting and its relationship to communities, he kept saying, "This is *why we're here*." This small phrase holds enormous meaning.

For Krushinsky and his colleagues, the phrase *why we're here* is first and foremost about public broadcasting's relationship to community. Public radio and television stations do not exist simply to gain audience share or recruit annual members to support them; rather, they are here, in our largest states and smallest towns, to serve communities. The stations are here so they can understand and illuminate a community's aspirations and concerns, engage people in the life of the community, and help people reengage and reconnect with one another.

They are here to fulfill a decidedly *public* mission.

Why we're here is also about location. It is about being in a particular place. Neal Hecker, Vice President for Programming at WPBT in Miami, tells us that his station is about "community television," which, for him, means being specifically focused on South Florida. Likewise, WSKG in Binghamton, New York, is about the state's Southern Tier.

This emphasis on location is especially important nowadays, for we live in a time when the health and notoriety of organizations is often gauged by their ability to extend beyond their original boundaries—to expand continually. But for each and every public broadcaster, being healthy and bold and ultimately relevant means something else—to put a stake in the ground about their commitment to their community. It means being rooted in a particular place, and developing a deep relationship with that community.

The notion of *why we're here* brings forward something else that those involved in public life all too often push aside—the deeply personal, even spiritual, part of this work. This small phrase speaks to our personal aspirations and the urge within us to create change beyond ourselves. *Why we're here* tells us something critical about the individuals in this work, and make no mistake: this is a story about individuals, each of whom took a chance to go down a path that differs sharply from the business-as-usual approach. It is a story about how each lived with the nagging risk of failure, how each individual found his or her own way, and how each discovered his or her own sense of possibility.

Together could they make a single declaration: we're here because we all believe that public broadcasting is essential to the life of our community.

Joe Krushinsky summed up the journey for many:

> *My sense of why we're here ties way back to trying to serve the public interest.... I wasn't in public media at the start. But I love to talk to people who were.... There were people who were just passionate about serving the public interest.... Over time, and it's easy to see how this would happen, it started to turn upside down, and we behaved as if we were here to make television—that television was the point.... The reason we're here is to leverage those technologies and platforms to serve the public interest. Never mind about the technology and the form, let's go back to figuring out what is that public interest we're trying to serve. And that sends us back to the community.*

This book documents how 12 public broadcasting stations and their staff turned outward toward their communities; transformed their ordinary, everyday efforts; contributed to the civic health of their communities; and declared with new clarity, "why we're here."

RICHARD C. HARWOOD AND AARON B. LEAVY

CHAPTER 1

WHERE TO NEXT?

We don't have a better way to exist. I mean, the industry itself has changed so much that if we are simply there to entertain as a broadcast channel and not be involved in our community, we might as well be programmed out of Seattle with offices in Los Angeles. The only reason to be where we are is to be involved in the space we're in. We're the Community Television Foundation of South Florida, that's our name. And the Community comes before the Television.

NEAL HECKER
VICE PRESIDENT FOR PROGRAMMING
WBPT, MIAMI

P ublic broadcasters face a critical choice these days, one that will define their relevance and significance for years to come. As the economy, the media landscape, and the nation's demographics all undergo radical change, will stations turn inward toward their organization or outward toward the community? There are some who say that the best route in today's conditions is simply to hunker down, find better ways to raise money, and weather the storm. This book is the story of 12 public broadcasting stations that considered this route, rejected it, and decided to take a less familiar path. It is the story of a dozen stations and their staffs that intentionally turned outward toward their communities and of the incredible results their efforts produced. Even more, this is the story about what the future of public broadcasting as a whole can be—and the story of the potential for any organization to turn outward and fulfill its public mission.

Charting a New Course

The summer of 2007 marked the 40TH anniversary of the Public Broadcasting Act of 1967,[1] which envisioned public broadcasters working in the community's interest. The Corporation for Public Broadcasting took the occasion to forge with the Harwood Institute for Public Innovation a collaboration called the Community Engagement Initiative (CEI), in which the institute would help 12 public radio and television stations meet two basic goals: improve the civic health of their communities and deepen their own local significance. For more than 20 years, the Harwood Institute, a

---

1 See pages 162-167 in the Appendices for excerpts from the Public Broadcasting Act of 1967 and President Johnson's signing statement.

nonprofit, nonpartisan, catalytic organization has inspired and guided people to step forward and take action rooted in their community and stay true to themselves. The institute works with individuals, organizations, and communities to turn outward and develop their ability to make more intentional choices and judgments that lead to impact. Drawing on the ideas, frameworks, and tools over two decades, the Community Engagement Initiative would seek to help public broadcasting stations do the same.

Scores of public television and radio stations applied to take part in the Initiative. An eclectic group of 12 stations were chosen—4 radio stations, 5 television stations, and 3 joint licensees. These stations served communities as small as Grand Marais, Minnesota, and as large and sprawling as Los Angeles, Miami, and Las Vegas.

Through CEI we set out to:

• **Generate 12 beacons of hope** within the public broadcasting system that could demonstrate what it means for stations to turn outward and engage communities in a new way;

• **Identify and articulate a clear set of ideas**, frameworks, messages, and tools that any and every public broadcasting station could use to make a difference in their community; and

• **Devise ways to spread this new approach** throughout the public broadcasting system. Contrary to many efforts, this was not about spreading so-called "best practices" or "step-by-step recipes" but rather about engaging individual stations in how they could re-orient themselves to communities and make their own choices and judgments about creating impact.

We came to CEI with an abiding belief that there is no one-size-fits-all approach for stations. Too many change efforts try to squeeze all newcomers into a prescribed approach that disregards their specific context, capacities, and potential. So, in this case, each station came to CEI with its own individual ideas and plans that it thought would contribute to local communities and that it wanted to expand upon or deepen through this initiative. Within each station, and across the Initiative, new ideas were tried, new approaches were generated, and unanticipated outcomes produced. Throughout CEI, stations worked closely with a coach deeply versed in Harwood ideas and frameworks. Stations participated in regular coaching calls to spur continued progress in their work. In addition, the stations came together periodically for intensive two- or three-day meetings—"workspaces," as we called them—in which they learned from each other; innovated together; shared promising practices; and integrated Harwood ideas, frameworks, and tools.

Obstacles in the Road

There was nothing easy about this work, and as with any change effort, there was no certainty of success. In essence, we were asking public broadcasters to reimagine their relationship with their communities, their connection to people. The broadcasters repeatedly had to consider and reconsider "why we're here." This produced dissonance, doubt, and even turmoil within individuals and stations. Our own experience is that change is not possible without such tumult. Indeed, turning outward required individuals and entire stations to examine their own mind-sets and practices—and the hidden, unrecognized assumptions that often guide what they say and do.

Furthermore, there were any number of structural and long-standing obstacles within individual stations and the larger public broadcasting system that threatened such an effort and that had to be confronted and squarely addressed. These obstacles, which are not unique to public broadcasters, included:

- **Rigid and "siloed" institutions:** Anyone who has worked with public broadcasting knows that individual stations can be highly fragmented institutions with each segment a self-contained "siloed" operation, which often makes it extremely difficult to work across various functions within stations and with the community.

- **The community as audience or passive donors:** Stations often view the local *community* as being synonymous with *audience* or, even more narrowly, as *members* and *donors*. When they look out their office windows, stations do not automatically see "dynamic communities" with a life all their own.

- **The habit of outreach:** Outreach in public broadcasting has usually meant a station selecting and producing programs and then finding ways to disseminate them to targeted audiences. Outreach of this sort is not the same as engagement, and changing this approach was more than just switching terms. To move from outreach to engagement would mean asking a station to rethink its purpose and its relationship to the community.

- **Deep suspicion of fads:** Public broadcasters have encountered one new fad after another, an experience that for good reason can leave them uncertain about true priorities and wary of new efforts. This is no small obstacle.

• **Tight money:** Like most public or civic sector organizations, public broadcasting stations face stiff competition for scarce dollars. Tight money can lead stations to turn inward, away from the community, as they try to harbor their funds. It also heightens skepticism about new ideas and approaches, as staff becomes increasingly risk averse.

Four Building Blocks for Turning Outward

The 12 CEI stations clearly had their work cut out for them. Our task was to help stations turn outward toward the community and create a sense of possibility so they could see for themselves how they could overcome long-standing challenges and create impact in the community. Without that reorientation, this effort would become just another one-off project. Even more, we had many station executives and staff members tell us that CEI would be too costly to stations and that when push came to shove the stations would abandon it. The approach would become just another fad, and as a result would fail like so many efforts before it. We were very conscious of these concerns.

To structure CEI, we used Harwood's Four Building Blocks for Turning Outward, a frame that guides our work with organizations and communities across the country:

1. **Know your community:** Creating real change requires that individuals and organizations working in communities be deeply rooted in those communities. To bring about change,

we must understand the context of our community and people's aspirations and concerns and how they talk about them. Our work must be relevant to people's lives and help them create new pathways back into community life. Otherwise, people become inputs for our own processes. Similarly, we must understand the *community's* capacity for change at any given moment. Otherwise, our plans and promises are simply window dressing.

2. **Focus on impact:** Having an impact means more than successfully implementing a program or initiative. It means addressing a specific public challenge or issue *and* creating the conditions for change at the same time. Without cultivating the leaders, networks, relationships, and norms of a community, we will be left with lots of programs but little community.

3. **Span boundaries:** Communities need more of what Harwood calls Boundary-Spanning Organizations,[2] groups that are able to hold up a mirror to the community so people can see their shared reality and shared aspirations. Similarly, we must create spaces within organizations where traditional department boundaries can be spanned and innovation can flourish.

4. **Cultivate public innovators:** Organizational and community change begins with individuals. These public innovators are catalysts for change. To create lasting change, these innovators

---

2 Boundary-Spanning Organizations (BSOS) are those which are able to cross traditional dividing lines in a community, incubate new ideas and spin them off, connect and convene groups that might otherwise never agree to get together, and hold up a mirror to the residents of a community so they can see their shared realities and aspirations. For more on BSOS see page 171 in the Appendices.

must stay connected to their aspirations for public life and to the urge to do good that initially drew them to this work.

Using these Four Building Blocks for Turning Outward, the 12 CEI stations, with Harwood, set out together.

CHAPTER 2

PROBLEMS
&
PROMISE

These communities are anxious for someone to pay attention to them, and they are thrilled that we, the public media station that they have consumed in their communities all along, suddenly is showing a genuine effort to be a part of their community and care about them.

MARK LEONARD
GENERAL MANAGER
ILLINOIS PUBLIC MEDIA

A S THE BROADCASTERS INVOLVED with CEI will tell you, their effort came along at a key moment for their stations—and for public broadcasting as a whole. Mark Leonard, General Manager for Illinois Public Media, put the problem this way: "We cannot deny that our model is either in jeopardy or broken." Another CEI participant, Amy Shaw, Vice President of Education Services at KETC in St. Louis, described the situation in terms of what worked once is not working any longer:

> CEI came along at just the right time, when some of the cataclysmic changes in the industry were making it apparent to some stations that things were going to have to change, that we couldn't rely on what we've been doing for much longer, and that now, in light of the global financial crisis, I think it's pretty apparent that we're not going to be able to do things in the way that we've always done them. It just doesn't work that way.

For Shaw and other CEI participants it soon became clear that the Harwood approach embedded in CEI would enable them to pursue an alternative to business-as-usual. None of the stations thought these changes would come easily. But once the initiative started, participants began sensing what they might achieve. At KETC in St. Louis, Amy Shaw knew that once she began down the CEI path she could not turn back:

> It's a little scary being a pioneer, not knowing where we're going or if anyone is following us, or if everyone as an industry is going to jump on board with this. But given the alternative, I think, we won't move forward successfully where we are now. We'll be

successful in the short term if we apply the same strategies that we've applied over the last 30 or 40 or 50 years, but we're not going to be successful in the long term. So I think the big bet for us is the success of our entire organization, the success of our community ... and to us engagement is really going to be the answer to that.

Kimberlie Kranich, Director of Community Engagement at Illinois Public Media, entered CEI with an acute awareness both of her station's and public broadcasting's separation from the community and the urgent need to do something about it. Within public broadcasting, Illinois Public Media has been considered among the leading practitioners of engaging the community. But for Kranich, the station was far less rooted in the community than it needed to be. She told us:

We're isolated right now to be honest. We're isolated, really we are. We think we know what the community needs are, and we try to program around those, but it became apparent that we don't have enough conversations outside—as a station collectively—to really know what the heck the needs are.

But once involved in CEI, Kranich, like Shaw and other participants, quickly sized up the vast potential before her:

There's going to be a shared understanding in our building among our staff about what the community needs are and what our role is in participating in meeting these public challenges. We don't have a shared knowledge right now. We're going to have one.

A Moment in Time for the Nation

CEI came about at a special moment in time for the nation, too. Then, as now, people are increasingly in search of ways to reconnect and reengage in public life and with one another. All across America, people are saying that they want to be a part of something larger than themselves; they want to make a difference. But let's be clear: abundant energy and opportunity does not make success automatic or even likely. Merely look over the span of American history, and you can count the lost opportunities at moments of hope for reconnection and reengagement. Simply consider the past decade to see opportunities lost: immediately after September 11 and then again after Hurricane Katrina, the window of opportunity for people to reconnect and reengage opened, only to quickly slam shut.

Once again, we face questions about who will people trust to create safe spaces for them to reengage and reconnect; who will they see as helping communities illuminate the tough issues we all must face together; and who will people believe are being effective in working to bring about positive impact in their communities? In short, who will people see as acting as *part of* their communities, as opposed to *apart* from them? The reality is that too many people still lack trust in too many leaders and institutions in their communities.

We believe that public television and radio stations are among a small group of institutions uniquely positioned to help communities move forward. Public broadcasters hold a deep reservoir of trust and good will in their communities. Their stations are one of the last standing boundary-spanning organizations that are able to bring people together across dividing lines. They can help incubate new ideas and spin them off. They can connect and convene groups that might otherwise never agree to get together, and then hold up a mirror to the residents of a community so they can see their shared realities and aspirations. Time and again, we have found in our work that public broadcasters are inherently less threatening than other civic organizations, rarely finding themselves in turf battles or funding conflicts. Even as public trust in leaders and institutions has faltered, public broadcasting stations remain trusted by communities.

Mark Leonard, General Manager of Illinois Public Media, reflected on this well-earned trust and the potential role of public broadcasting stations in spanning boundaries:

> We have way more equity in our public trust than we can imagine. No one thinks that we have an ulterior motive.... The accumulated good will has been tremendous. The rarity of boundary-spanning organizations—the organization that is able to demonstrate a self-lessness and the willingness and ability to pull together people and organizations on behalf of community need—there is a desire for that, and not many are seen as being able to provide it.

Communities Are Waiting

Many of the station leaders we worked with wondered whether their communities would embrace public broadcasters stepping out into the community and playing a new role. Would the community be willing to engage with the station? Would the community ultimately trust the station? At every CEI station, in every community, the answer came back clearly and unequivocally, "Yes!" Mark Leonard put his experience this way:

I think we're realizing ... that these communities are anxious for someone to pay attention to them, and they are thrilled that we, the public media station that they have consumed in their communities all along, suddenly is showing a genuine effort to be a part of their community and care about them.

Time after time, station leaders reported that when they moved outside their station walls, they were met by a community enthusiastic about their work. In Binghamton, for instance, an individual at one community meeting responded to station leaders who had wondered aloud whether their vision for a more engaged station made sense. "If not you," the person said, "who?" And followed up the remark by asking, "When can you get started?"

When Maryland Public Television scheduled a community meeting, it worried that the station would have to cancel for a lack of public interest. Would anyone bother to come? Instead, it faced a dramatically different problem—the number of people who wanted to come far outstripped the size of the room.

People in communities eagerly responded when the CEI stations talked about their new roles in the community. KNPR, the public radio station for Las Vegas and the sprawling territory of southern Nevada, found that once it made clear to the community that its established *State of Nevada* program would focus more on locally relevant issues, people began to hold the station accountable for its promise. Now, when *State of Nevada* veers too far away from addressing topics of local significance, KNPR's phone lines light up as listeners remind the station of its pledge to the community.

A different version of the same community awareness is happening at KETC in St. Louis, reports Amy Shaw, Vice President of Education Services. People are recognizing that changes are taking place in her station's programming.

More people in the community are saying, "Something's happening here. I don't know what it is, but something's happening." Sort of being the organization they always thought we could be, or that to some people we were, but it was sort of reinforcing why we were that organization, or recapturing in their heart who we were, and why they liked us.

We have found similar sentiments beyond the realm of public broadcasting in other communities across the country where people are waiting for community groups and organizations to step forward, span boundaries, and authentically engage. Bottom line, this is about organizations turning outward, which at its most fundamental level is about an organization recreating its relationship with its community. For public broadcasters, making such a turn came not a moment too soon—the need is critical, the opportunity abundant, and the public ready.

Change in the Face of Challenges

In the chapters of this book, you'll read about some of the many changes the 12 stations of CEI made, the impact of their work within the community, and how they managed to do what they did. You'll read about how the CEI stations turned outward and reimagined their programs to make what one broadcaster called "a philosophical shift" in what they do and why they do it. You'll learn how stations used social media to create new community platforms and how they became a sought-after partner and a trusted convenor. You'll hear from CEI leaders how their stations shifted their focus from activity to action, from process to impact, and from programs to community.

At a time when many organizations in communities have turned inward—focusing first and foremost on their own operations, brands, plans, and governance, a focus that cannot improve the civic health of a community or deepen a station's local significance—the most critical initial step for each station was to turn outward. You'll see that by turning outward stations also generated the momentum for developing new *internal* practices that could support their new approach. It is tempting to misread this insight, as turning outward runs counter to many internal organizational-change approaches. But the CEI stations confirmed what we have seen in organizations and communities for more than 20 years: to create deep internal change, turn outward. Indeed, the essential lesson here is that for internal changes to be effective, they *must* be grounded in a philosophical and strategic imperative that only comes from forging a new relationship with the community.

Follow the Money

You will remember that at the outset of this initiative many onlookers thought that the CEI broadcasters would give up trying to turn outward and change when the money pressures became too big. Financial pressures, they said, would be stronger than any idea of engaging with the community. The fact is that economic pressures only worsened during the time of CEI. In the middle of this effort, the housing market imploded, banks collapsed, and the nation entered an historic recession. Surely now these stations would abandon this work in favor of the tried and true, right?

Some CEI participants were worried about this too. Joe Krushinsky at Maryland Public Television, admits that, like many in the public broadcasting system, he wondered whether CEI would be able to survive in a tough economy:

If you had asked me at the start what might be some of the things that could make this project go badly, or end prematurely that [unprecedented financial stress] would have been pretty close to the top of the list. If we run into hard times people will run screaming from this. And focus on short-term survival.

But the results tell a different story. For nearly every station, including Krushinsky's, the work that emerged as part of CEI became a *profit center.* Time and again, we heard—and continue to hear—from stations that it was their CEI work that led them to raise more money than ever before. Becoming relevant and significant wasn't too costly. Just the reverse: it was profitable!

To be clear, we have often said to stations (and other organizations involved in such work) that the ideas and principles of turning outward that we advocate should *not* be used for fundraising purposes—that is, as a ploy for raising new funds. But we also say that, for those organizations that do turn outward and become more relevant and significant in their communities, new support almost always follows. For each of the CEI stations, it did. Here are just a handful of examples:

• At a time when state support was cut, Illinois Public Media's success in turning outward generated a 28 percent increase in funding from local contributors. What's more, before leading his station through CEI, General Manager Mark Leonard often spoke about how difficult it was to get the attention of young entrepreneurs, let alone their support. Now, he reports, the same entrepreneurs who once avoided his calls are seeking him out and engaging with the station. And just before this book was completed, Leonard contacted us to say that his station had just won the Overall Development Award, the highest award given by the PBS Development Advisory Committee, and that "our award-winning entry was based largely on our engagement activities with the Harwood Institute." From the station's winning entry:

> The work we did with the CPB-funded Harwood Community Engagement Initiative provided the backdrop. It's work that continues today and will help to make us not just successful, but a significant community organization in the years ahead.... [The station] had its most successful year ever in total annual giving. We see community engagement principles as one of the keys for continued growth in the years to come.

• Maryland Public Television's work with CEI helped spur an individual donor to contribute $1 million for a New Initiatives Fund to support future community-based initiatives like CEI. Discussing still another emerging effort, Joe Krushinsky says, "We don't even have a product yet, and two foundations have committed money to move forward."

• From both local and national sources, more than $2 million has been invested in KETC of St. Louis to sustain CEI-related efforts. KETC's work with the community prompted The Dana Brown Charitable Trust to donate $1 million to enable the station to renovate a section of its building to create a new space for ongoing community engagement.

• In 2008, Wells Fargo Foundation cut funding for every single one of its grantees in Las Vegas, except for KNPR, whose CEI-inspired work on its *Community Connections* program was seen as too valuable to cut. Instead of cutting back, Wells Fargo increased KNPR's funding.

• In Grand Marais, Minnesota, the public radio station WTIP recently completed its most successful membership drive ever. WTIP's *More than Radio* membership effort reflected the station's new relationship with the community. The drive featured listeners, community leaders, and nonprofit managers celebrating their partnerships with WTIP and expressing the station's value in the community. Since starting CEI, WTIP's membership has increased by nearly 30 percent.

• As a result of its CEI work, WSKG in Binghamton, New York, received $150,000 from the Conrad and Virginia Klee Foundation for a *Working on Wellness Initiative* and is now part of CPB's STEM community-engagement initiative, with two grants of $25,000 and $10,000. General Manager Brian Sickora sees the connection between CEI and fundraising clearly, "All of our revenue lines are up, our major donors have just about doubled, pledge is up. That was helpful to show to the staff, that 'this stuff might actually pay off.'"

The Promise

The promise of this approach is straightforward: by turning

outward, public broadcasting stations can improve the civic health of their communities and deepen their local significance—thereby re-creating their relationship with their communities. This aim wasn't just a rhetorical notion, or some new slogan. Nor, as we noted, was CEI a best-practice approach to be blindly installed or even a recipe to be followed step by step. Fulfilling the promise of CEI required stations to make choices and judgments all along their paths for change. Further, such choices never end, as new challenges arise, context changes, and capacity varies. The change these stations created was hard won; nothing was automatic. But these 12 stations demonstrated how it happens.

CHAPTER 3

THE ORGANIZATION- FIRST APPROACH

Many of the people who work in the social sector don't like the public. Why would you engage someone you don't respect?

COMMUNITY-BASED ORGANIZATION LEADER

We know what works. The challenge is convincing the community what works.

NATIONAL ORGANIZATION LEADER

BEFORE MOVING ON TO the full story of the 12 public broadcasting stations, we want to step back and discuss with greater depth the problems of inwardness and their implications. For, as we have repeatedly said, the challenges and conditions facing CEI stations mirror those we have seen in communities and organizations across the country. The basic difference is that the CEI stations met the challenges.

In this chapter, we draw in particular from a Harwood Institute research report done in collaboration with the Kettering Foundation, *The Organization-First Approach*, in which we initially documented the strong inward impulse in organizations. The research followed nearly a dozen organizations over a two-year period in which we engaged in observations, in-depth interviews, and conversations about their engagement with communities. At the core of the report is a simple idea: public-minded organizations of all sorts face a common challenge in seeing the relevance of engaging communities both to their work and, more important, to their mission.

Most noteworthy among our findings is that, despite impulses to turn outward, many leaders and their organizations find themselves in a profound grip of inwardness in which their work is defined in terms of the needs and interests of their organizations, not those of the community. We found that even those groups that try to buck inwardness face deep challenges in terms of the expectations, funding, emphasis on professionalism, and measures of success that dominate their world and operations.

Organizational Success Is Priority One

Foremost in the minds of most leaders is the health and vibrancy of their organizations. Of course, on one level, this makes sense.

But when stability itself becomes the goal, its effects can lead to inwardness. We could see this plainly among those organizations with local affiliates and members. One leader explained to us that her top priority is enabling state chapters to develop "their core functions," which include "having a business plan to establish resources, 501(c)(3) status, board [recruiting], that sort of thing." Another leader described the core competencies for their affiliates in this way: "Board management, defined programs, fundraising." As you can see, in both instances, there was little mention of outward, community goals.

Internal operations are also the predominant frame of reference for leaders of locally based organizations. As one leader of a local grant-making organization said, "My first priority when I got here was to make sure we have the right people on staff." In practice, this means that making such staff changes often becomes a prerequisite—a precondition—for working in communities. We encountered the same pressure time and again in our efforts with the 12 CEI stations. And yet, as you'll come to see, once the public broadcasting stations were able to turn outward intentionally, it was their community focus that became the driving force behind significant internal changes, and not the other way around.

When asked to describe the role they play in communities, most leaders in our study were apt to talk about the programs they implement, services they provide, and constituents they represent; few included the community's health, their connection, or engagement with it. One leader put it this way, "We're a program organization." He then added, "We have a very specific goal. We work with communities that want to adopt our programs!" In our work with CEI stations, we initially found a similar notion sounded by many public broadcasters, who said that their primary mission is to create and broadcast television and radio programs. Again, the health and development of the community itself did not come up. Many organizations use the word *readiness* when talking about communities. What they mean by the term is whether a community is ready to adopt the organization's program or services!

Many organization leaders told us their focus on programs derives from their funding, which is tied almost exclusively to program expansion and implementation. Thus, they develop staff as program managers because their funding stream requires them to deliver on programs; and they reproduce programs from one community to the next because funders say they want to replicate successful initiatives. "There are few grant RFPS [Requests for Proposals] for engagement or community building work," said one organization leader. "It is very difficult to develop capacities [engagement] when funding is all about the delivery of programs."

These financial incentives often narrow or define the role that organization leaders believe they can afford to play, or should play, in communities. As one leader put it, "We're not really in a position to play a broader community building role. No one wants to fund us to do that."

Organizations with a successful program model feel tremendous pressure to further grow these programs—and to do it quickly. "We're hot right now," explained one leader representing a youth-oriented organization. "People want to fund us to come to their communities. The feeling in our organization is that we may not stay hot forever—so we've got to grow!" He concluded by saying, "I'm not sure if we're a good fit in every community, but the money says, 'Go!'"

Some organization leaders even suggest they feel bullied by funders to expand their programs and services whether or not a given community is a good fit for the program. One leader of a group working on health-care issues said, "We don't really even ask if our programs are right for a community. Instead, we ask, 'Where do we think we can get our programs adopted?'" His organization was under a mandate from a key funder to reach specific expansion quotas, which became the ultimate priority for the organization rather than making an impact on the communities it served.

The way leaders are evaluated further promotes their intense focus on their organizational needs and interests, even when both are out of sync with their communities. Several leaders told us that grant and board evaluations rarely include any notions of their relationship with the community, beyond the effective spread of their programs. This is a trend we see nationwide. One leader, who summarized the conditions facing most organizations, gave voice to the concern saying, "I'm not evaluated by how well I involve people. Keeping my job depends on what we get done."

Many of the leaders we interviewed also describe how difficult it is to demonstrate a connection between community engagement and their impact in communities. "Until we can show impact," said one leader, "no one cares. It's just process." This, too, was something we heard repeatedly from public broadcasters. As you'll see, the CEI stations were able to address this concern head on and demonstrate the benefits from engaging with communities.

Even leaders who believe engaging communities is essential to their work were hesitant to make engagement a priority within their own organizations. One leader who talked at length about how engagement is pivotal to the success of her work in communities, quickly added, "I would get fired if I told people I was doing engagement." Another leader said, "Even when I'm doing engagement, I don't necessarily tell people that's what I'm doing!" And yet another leader added, "I'll be frank; engagement is not something I'm going to go to the mat for. It's just not worth it."

Pursuit of The Organization-First Approach

Below are four steps that, among others, organizations tend to pursue as they implement an Organization-First Approach. As we examine the work of the CEI stations, you will see how they created alternate paths rooted in their stations turning outward.

1. **A Reliance on Expert Knowledge:** The first step is to pinpoint community needs and interests This work often begins with staff members examining various expert-driven data to help identify critical community needs and best practices. Leaders see this step as critical for defining how to tailor their work to a community and what to emphasize in their effort to "educate" and bring along the community (see next two steps). One leader explained the importance of this step in this way, "We begin our work with a needs assessment, asset-mapping, and gap analysis. We figure out what a community can do for itself and where they can use our help. This drives our decision-making."

2. **Educate the Community:** The next step is to enlist community members to support a specific organizationally defined course of action, volunteer to help with a program, or encourage different organizations to cooperate with one another. Here,

organization leaders often express the desire for community members to "buy in" to the organization's vision for action. As one leader explained, "We've done extensive research on how to address this need. We bring on board those who are ready [to work on this need] through a process of education." Another leader expressed a similar point of view. "There's no reason for communities to reinvent the wheel," he said. "We've learned what works on these issues and we try to make sure people [learn our lessons]." Organization leaders indicate that they try to reach out to as many people as possible so that their message is heard and they can push their organizational agenda.

3. **Implementation Planning:** A third step is to ensure that a core group of key community members are committed to a clear set of action strategies. One leader explained that when her organization engages a community, "We go over scientifically based research for a number of different strategies. Then we ask people, 'Which of these strategies do you want to use?'" Here, key community leaders are asked to select from existing strategies chosen by the organization to implement a preset initiative or program. While such planning occasionally involves the general community, more often the organizations seek out participation from the leaders and service providers who they believe should be involved in the program or initiative. The organization leaders with whom we talked expressed frustration with broader community engagement, believing that involving the public requires more work and greater risk.

4. **Collaboration:** This last step typically involves the same cadre

of people from the previous three steps. Leaders are resistant to including new people because it may lead to questioning of their plan and derail progress. Here, the relevant organizations and stakeholders gather to make agreements about which organization will do what. Some of the organization leaders with whom we spoke also describe collaboration as the most difficult step of engagement. "It's so hard to keep agreements," one leader told us. "The players [in the participating organizations] change, people adopt new priorities. It's really hard."

Risks of Deeper Engagement

Few of the organization leaders we interviewed considered deliberation—that is, people coming together to consider issues and weigh choices and trade-offs—as a viable strategy for working with communities. When pressed, most describe deliberation as an unwieldy endeavor, fraught with many potential pitfalls. Many suggested that sponsoring deliberation would run counter to their role in communities. And when pressed to further examine the possibility of using deliberation in their work, most leaders' definition of the term grew so broad that it included any time *any* group of people make a decision.

Another risk for many leaders is the intense pressure they feel to represent a particular point of view when they do engage with the community. We found this is especially true for constituent-based organizations.

One leader of an advocacy-based organization explained, "Our job is to represent a specific viewpoint. By definition, we can't lead a deliberative process. We can be at the table to represent the view of our members, but we can't lead the process." This leader went

on to say that if the organization took a neutral role in a deliberative process it would lose allies. "The people we work with would
consider it a betrayal if we didn't stand up strongly for our views."

Leaders of program-based organizations feel a similar
pressure. Professionals who have worked on an issue for years
have often come to their own conclusion about best practices and
are understandably invested both personally and professionally
in those conclusions. To them, if the outcome of working with
the community is something that doesn't heed established best
practices, then it is misguided or misinformed. Worse still, such
an outcome would erode the organization's credibility among
colleagues. As one leader told us, "We know what works. The
challenge is convincing the community what works."

What we find is that leaders in organizations across the coun
try are anxious about opening up spaces in which conversations
are neither controlled nor directed. Doing so risks incorporating
new variables and slowing progress toward a manageable, specific
solution. Opening up the process runs counter to one of the critical goals leaders often seek from engaging their communities:
"We need to know that we're going to come out of [the meeting]
with agreements for who is going to do what." For many, engaging with the public is a process to gain buy in, assign roles, and
advance their programs.

Stepping back, there seems to be an underlying "fear of the
public" that is present among many organizational leaders. "The
political stakes go way up," said one leader in our study about
convening everyday people in communities. He continued,
"People who are important to [the organization] might not like
the results." Many of the organization leaders we interviewed said
that the potential pay-off is far too low and the potential risks

far too high for them to pursue. Another leader said, "Either nothing happens or people become divisive. Either way, the organization that sponsored the process gets the blame. We can't afford to take that kind of risk."

Here are the types of "risk questions" organization leaders consider in deciding whether, or how, to be involved with a deliberative process:

• *Can we afford to be associated with the outcome of the deliberative process?*

• *Can we commit to the choices people make in the process if we disagree?*

• *How will our allies or key constituents perceive us if we sign on to the outcomes of a deliberative process? Can we risk the potential of alienating them?*

• *Who will we have to work with in the wake of the deliberative process? Do we want to be associated with these groups?*

• *Will the process serve the organization's needs and interests?*

Another risk is the increased expectations that come with sponsoring this kind of effort. Many leaders tell us they worry that sponsoring community conversations or engaging the community in other ways carries an implicit expectation for follow-up work—much of which may be beyond the mission of their organization and most certainly beyond its capacities. "The organization that sponsors deliberation is expected to take responsibility for implementing the ideas that come out of this process," explained one organization leader. "It is sometimes possible to get funding to do [a deliberative process]," said another leader, "but it is very difficult to get funding to do any follow-up work. There seems to be an expectation among funders that whatever the community comes up with we can do that work in addition to what we're already doing."

Barriers to a Community Orientation

We asked leaders in our study to consider what it would take for their organizations and others around them to shift to more of a community orientation, and they identified five common challenges, all of which echo concerns we hear throughout our work with organizations and leaders—and which were barriers within our CEI work.

1. Is Engaging the Community Within Our Responsibilities?

How organizations answer this question drives how they will make decisions about their approach to turning outward. Organizations that see their primary responsibilities solely as promoting an issue or a particular point of view, implementing a program, or providing services seem locked into the Organization-First Approach. On the other hand, organizations that view "community change" as one of their primary responsibilities are in a better position to approach engagement with a community-first orientation.

Here one leader described the way her grant-making organization changed its sense of responsibility in its approach to working with the community and the public. "We used to think our job was done after we distributed money. Then we blamed the grant recipients if nothing happened," she said. It was her organization's shift toward accepting greater responsibility for community results—that is, seeing its job as related to the health of the community rather than merely granting dollars—that changed how they worked with and engaged with the community.

Another leader explained a similar shift in her organization, which initially could have been described as a funding intermediary. "We would assess needs [in the community], raise and distribute money, and then do an evaluation at the end of the grant cycle to see what happened." Regardless of the results of their efforts, the organization would basically repeat the same process the next year. Then the change came. "No more," she said. "We decided that we have to take responsibility for community results." She explained that it's not enough to distribute money. The shift away from distributing money to claiming greater responsibility for seeking to create an impact, changed how the organization works with, and engages, the community.

2. Do We Have Credibility?

Organization leaders raised three specific concerns about whether their organizations even have the standing to take a lead role in engaging their communities.

• **Expectations.** Is engagement a role people expect our organization to play? As one leader remarked, "People expect us to do what we've always done. If we were going to do more in the way of engagement, it would take us time to have the credibility."

• **Competency.** A second aspect of credibility relates to these organizations' core competencies. That is, can the organization do a credible job of organizing, facilitating, and following up on engagement work?

• **Mission.** The third aspect of credibility raised by organization leaders relates to the role each organization has chosen for itself. For instance, organizations that have chosen to speak out on behalf of a specific constituency believe they have limited options in pursuing engagement activities. As one leader we quoted earlier put it, "If we're not representing our point of view, we lose credibility." More generally, as one leader of an education-focused organization said, "I don't know if we think we have the right to do this." Another leader expressed a similar sentiment when speaking about her board: "There is quite a bit of ambivalence. People say, 'It's not our place.'"

3. Who Will Lead this Work Internally?

The leaders with whom we spoke listed several internal barriers to expanding their organization's role in leading community engagement. A lack of funding was typically the first obstacle they mentioned; the lack of appropriate skills was second; for others, internal interest presented yet another barrier.

Leaders told us there is no line item in their budgets for engaging the community. Budgets, they said, are built to support program activities, so engagement efforts require leaders to "borrow" time, money, and staff from other budgets.

Describing his organization's lack of engagement skills, one leader said, "We don't have the people who know how to do this."

Another leader explained, "Running conversations is an art, and we don't have the people who have those skills... We hire people to run programs." Lacking internal capacity, leaders saw consultants as the most realistic approach for securing the necessary community engagement skills. One leader put it simply: "We need consultants." According to one leader who wanted to develop her staff's engagement skills, "There aren't grant dollars to support that kind of training." But, as you'll see later, for many CEI stations developing their skills didn't require extra funds or additional consultants—and ultimately helped differentiate the stations within their communities.

Beyond funding and skills, some leaders point to a lack of interest in engagement within their organizations. Additionally, few of the individuals interested in engagement have the organizational support or standing to promote and sustain engagement as a core practice.

4. Where Is the Public to Engage?

Many of the leaders suggested that ever-increasing social mobility and fragmentation, as well as modern lifestyles and reliance on the Internet, make it harder to engage people in their communities. Some leaders describe an increasingly "elusive public." One leader asked rhetorically, "How do you engage people when you can't make physical contact?... People work two jobs, they don't go to their neighborhood schools, they pull into their garage after work." Another leader asked, "I wonder if engagement is from the world of our fathers? People don't have time for this now. It's harder to dedicate time so they retreat away from community."

Organization leaders in high-growth regions of the country

attributed the difficulty in reaching people to the transient lifestyle in their communities. One leader described the trends in his community in this way: "Ninety-seven percent of people weren't born in the state. Thirty-two percent have been here less than five years." Others described similar statistics or scenarios for their own communities. These leaders wondered whether higher social mobility was leading to civic indifference. "People are so mobile around here they don't feel vested," is how one leader put it.

Conversely, organization leaders working in communities with stagnant or declining growth found the public elusive for a different reason. "People in these communities have been through a lot. They can be a little jaded about whether [becoming engaged] is worth the effort."

While some leaders remained doggedly determined in their efforts to find new or more effective ways to work with the public, frustration with a transient population or a population beset by stagnating growth led many to doubt whether it was realistic or possible to engage a meaningful number of people. Some leaders concluded that it was easier to stay focused on implementing programs than to invest the time, effort, and resources in trying to find a public that might never materialize. As one leader said, "You end up reaching out to people who you know will be there and who will stay there."

5. Where's the Proof?

Time and again, these leaders returned to their need to be able to draw direct links between community engagement, action, and demonstrable results. For these leaders, the need to prove to funders, their boards, and others that their efforts yield measurable results undermined their willingness to explore further or different approaches to engagement.

"I can't prove that [engagement] is a good return on investment," explained one leader. Another leader added that the challenge in promoting engagement is that there aren't good stories about how engagement leads to positive impact in communities. "We lack examples about how this might play out," he said. "We encourage our chapters to get involved with the community, but we can't tell them what the benefits will be." Still another leader said that organizations were evaluated strictly by outcomes, "People don't really care about process. They only want to know what you've done." And, "Until we can show impact, no one cares. It's just process." One leader was quite blunt in our conversations about different approaches to community engagement. Midway through the conversations she said, "This is not my style. I like to get things done."

Indeed, many of the leaders we interviewed have built their reputations inspiring others to take action. They talk about experiencing a rush from accomplishing goals no one thought could be accomplished. What's more, the drive not to fail is an equally powerful motivator, which prompts some leaders to rush to action. As one leader said, "There is a whole lot of ego tied up in showing you've got it together and know how to get things done."

Many of the CEI stations faced similar pressure to demonstrate results. They also realized that their relevance and significance was in jeopardy if they remained inward facing.

Overcoming Inwardness—There is another Way

It is not that this focus on programs, strategic planning, fundraising, impact measurement, and other activities is unnecessary; in fact, quite the opposite could be argued. Each of these elements is essential to a healthy organization.

But what if the unintended consequences of such an inward focus take organizations further from the very communities they seek to serve? What if the programs and initiatives they seek to implement are actually disconnected from people's everyday aspirations and concerns? Indeed, what if the very incentives and structures being used reward such inwardness to the exclusion of turning outward to communities and people?

The Harwood Institute's experience is that it is possible to create pathways for organizations and leaders to turn outward; in fact, we know it is. The chapters that follow will trace the work of 12 CEI stations and demonstrate that, while the pressures to turn inward are pervasive and the Organization-First Approach may be common, there is another way.

CHAPTER 4

TURN OUTWARD

I hope that this work means that we're coming out of some mid-life challenges for public television. We kind of lost our way. We struggled, funding was challenging from a number of directions, and in some ways, our business practices faltered. We were more concerned with the bottom line next quarter and next year than our relevance in the community and our service. As soon as we can reorient ourselves and keep our eye on the ball, so to speak, in terms of public service, I think the support from all sectors will come.

JOE KRUSHINSKY
VICE PRESIDENT FOR INSTITUTIONAL ADVANCEMENT
MPT, MARYLAND

L IKE LEADERS IN SO many organizations, those in public broadcasting confront enormous pressure to look
inward—to focus on creating still one more strategic plan
or undertaking yet another rebranding effort or rearranging their
organization chart once more. Such inwardness is prevalent among
groups and organizations across the country, including, in our experience, United Ways, community foundations, public libraries,
and other institutions that claim a civic-minded mission.

Many public broadcasters recognize the need for change in
their stations and communities. But recognizing it and making it
real are two entirely different matters. Listening to CEI leaders, it
is clear that only by seeing their communities in a new way were
they able to do their work in a new way. This shift in orientation
is essential. Without seeing the community differently, there is no
impetus to radically change what one does. For the 12 CEI stations,
this reorientation came from the process of turning outward.

In fall 2008, Patricia Harrison, the Chief Executive Officer of the
Corporation for Public Broadcasting, asked Richard Harwood to
speak at a series of round-robin conferences in which public television executives take part. During these meetings, Harrison posed
the following challenge to public broadcasters: What would you do
if you had to cut your budget by 15 to 40 percent? Mind you, her
challenge came before the full brunt of the economic recession had
taken hold. Over the course of three hours, small groups engaged
in lively give-and-take. But when one listened closely to these conversations, it was clear that their energy was focused inward. Much
of the discussions revolved around how stations could protect their
funding, their turf, and their audience.

When it was Rich's turn to speak, he made the observation that
while the mission of public broadcasting is to serve communities

(remember, *public* is in their name), relatively few of the conversations touched on a station's relationship with community. Instead, the conversations focused on how stations could incrementally cut budgets, identify more appealing membership gifts for on-air pledge drives, and create stronger marketing campaigns. The essence of holding a *public* mission seemed lost, cast aside in the rush to survive. And yet, it is at such times when clarity about one's public mission is most needed.

Knowing the powerful and pervasive inward pull experienced by organizations, we began our work in the Community Engagement Initiative by focusing our efforts on helping the stations develop a different mind-set and cultivate practices that support an outward orientation. Instead of stations following the usual reaction of turning inward in the face of tension or pressure—or even in the midst of new opportunities—we wanted them to turn outward toward the community.

Turning outward was one of the "core disruptions" in CEI that created the conditions for change among the stations. It required stations to develop a new notion about their relationships with their communities, to recognize that they would need different perspectives and practices to fulfill that new relationship and that they would need to become more intentional in making choices and judgments in their work.

Amy Shaw at KETC in St. Louis spoke of the importance of turning outward and the centrality of the idea for the station going forward:

We embedded this idea of turning outward in our strategic-planning process, so that it was something that lived on not just as an idea or a project. I think in public television we tend to see things

as projects. And it became pretty apparent that this was more than
a project. Community engagement is not a project....It's about how
we're thinking about who we are in relationship to our community
and how we'll be viewed—who we'll be in the future, basically.

Turning Outward Starts with Shared Aspirations

In some ways turning outward was actually a *return* for these
public broadcasters in that it helped them to reconnect with the
very reasons they joined public broadcasting. Turning outward
gave them a kind of permission to act on their original aspirations
for what public broadcasting could be. These aspirations included
the desire to make a difference in the communities where they live
and to be more relevant to those communities.

From the outset, we asked public broadcasters to talk explicitly
about their aspirations because we know that people, whether in
public broadcasting or any other civic-related endeavor, often lose
sight of their aspirations over time. Too often people's aspirations
are pushed aside, devalued, or caked over in the layers of bureaucra-
cy and the daily grind of work. And yet, when people turn outward,
it is their aspirations that provide them with the fuel and guidance
for moving ahead. It is when people can articulate their aspirations
that the reorientation we talk about gains currency.

The focus on the kind of community that public broadcasters
wanted to create through their work rooted in CEI is something
very real for them. Station leaders spoke of the focus on aspirations as unlocking something they didn't know they had lost or a
way to give voice to long-held beliefs that had been pushed aside.
Kimberlie Kranich of Illinois Public Media, described her work in
public media as profoundly personal:

This is a calling, that's a spiritual practice that I get paid to do in the realm of media and community. To be able to combine my passion for the underdog, my passion for introspection, my passion for how do things work and how can we make them work better, and being able to use media toward that goal—just fit me.

Joe Krushinsky, at Maryland Public Television, found that CEI enabled him to express and name his long-held beliefs about the power and potential of public broadcasting:

This process has been good for me because I have always instinctively had a notion that public broadcasting could do this kind of good work and have this kind of impact on the community. But this has given me the language to describe it.

Sometimes simply opening up a space within the station to consider aspirations proved powerful in itself. Nancy Dobbs, General Manager at KRCB in Sonoma County, California, tells the story of a veteran staff member whom everyone had expected to rail against "soft" conversation topics, such as aspirations. But when Dobbs held conversations about the role of the station in the community, she said she heard perspectives she'd never expected, particularly in the response from that long-time staffer, who said: "I have been waiting for this conversation for 60 years."

For KRCB, a focus on aspirations enabled people at the station to find shared interests and opened a space where staff could talk about the kind of community and station it wanted to create rather than the kind of programming it sought to broadcast. Talking about aspirations revealed a yearning across the staff to do things differently—a yearning few could have identified before CEI.

At WPBT in Miami, the station's Vice President for Programming, Neal Hecker, much like Dobbs in Sonoma County, found that talking about aspirations helped people discover what they held in common and helped create a shared sense of the direction they needed to move as a station. He also found that a focus on aspirations enabled his staff to stay focused on impact—the effect on the community—rather than simply on programming:

> *The thing about aspirations, and that's maybe at the heart of all this, is that it gives you the open door, the common ground. Not "What is it we want to do in a half hour of television?" It's "What do you want to accomplish? What is it that you want to see happen?" Everything, the whole conversation shifts 180 degrees. It's no longer about just doing stuff, it's about changing stuff.*

We find that without a discussion of aspirations, it is hard to turn outward and identify the right trajectory for moving ahead. Without such a discussion, almost everything people mention can seem reasonable and doable; almost everything can seem to be legitimately in play. As a result efforts become unfocused and haphazard. Aspirations ground the conversation and make it real for people. By articulating their aspirations, people identify and name what they value most and why. And in the end, it is these aspirations that they will go to bat for.

It's All about Impact

Truth be told, we wanted stations to turn outward not just

to reconnect with their aspirations but so they could make a difference in the community—have an impact. We wanted them to make their aspirations *real*. Otherwise, their efforts would have been an academic exercise, which would have been quickly snuffed out and rejected, seen as just another fad. This meant that stations had to rediscover and rethink their potential for creating impact in the community. Everything they did needed to pay some impact dividend.

By creating a focus on community impact, CEI opened up a new way of thinking and acting for stations. They moved from seeing themselves as producers of programming to generators of new possibilities for leveraging their assets, in different combinations and with different partners, to improve the civic health of their communities. The focus on community impact became the anchor for station efforts, keeping staff focused on the larger goals at hand. Absent this focus, stations would slide back into internally focused business-as-usual.

This relentless insistence on community impact helped change the conversation about station priorities and push station staff to rethink long-held assumptions. Rather than hoping that myriad activities added up to impact, station staff began to see the goal of community impact as a way to turn their efforts toward meaningful action. Take Illinois Public Media, whose focus on community impact led the staff to begin to talk about the station in a fundamentally different way. Director of Internet Development, Jack Brighton, captured the change this way: "We're a media organization that changes our community for the better. We're about making an impact." The station's General Manager, Mark Leonard, went a step further: "Now our projects start in the community, not in our conference room."

Leonard went on to describe the station's new approach to any new efforts, saying, "We ask, 'How will we impact the community?'"

For Kelly Luoma, the Station Programmer for Vermont Public Television, the focus on community impact prompted her to evaluate the likely effect of projects, programs, and partnerships in a new way. This meant finding a clear sense of purpose, one that was tied to the community, not just the station. Turning outward and seeking community impact required her station to make more choices and judgments, not fewer. She put it this way:

> *To find the impact means you really have to have some sense of what you're trying to accomplish by creating content or creating engagement. It's not just doing something to do it; it's really trying to think things through in much more depth than we ever have before ... being ruthlessly strategic, and making sure that what we take on is truly strategic, and we understand why we're getting involved. This has really made us think differently, think far more strategically, think far more about the impact of taking on projects, work, and partnerships.*

What Luoma's quote makes clear is that setting community impact as a clear goal means that the station, in a word, has to be *focused*. As she says, "It's not just doing something to do it."

Putting the focus on impact and not simply on going through the motions helped change the conversation in many of the CEI stations. Turning outward and seeking community impact fundamentally alters the conversation. People now must explore and articulate their intention and purpose.

At KETC, in St. Louis, a focus on creating community impact prompted the station to develop a formal statement about the kind of questions it should consider when doing its daily work. KETC wrote an updated strategic plan that was heavily influenced by their CEI involvement. The updated plan stated:

> We seek to focus outward, to leverage our reservoir of trust and integrity to provide pathways to strengthen the civic health of our region. To that end, we are considering the questions that frame the Community Engagement Initiative:

> • How can KETC's community-engagement efforts become better linked to daily operations?

> • How can our efforts lead to greater community significance, where KETC is more involved and engaged in the community?

> • How can our efforts lead communities to view KETC as a trusted and essential leader?

> • How will the public challenges in our region get addressed through our approach to our work?

> • How can we strengthen our community?

You can see that these questions focus squarely on community impact. The station realized that if it was to turn outward and have community impact, it needed to create a set of questions very different than those that previously had guided its activities.

Focus on Innovation and Creating

By turning outward, these station leaders could see new possibilities for their work, their stations, and, perhaps most important, their relationships with their communities. But embracing these new possibilities would require stations to do more than just shift their orientation: they had to innovate and create.

In the past, stations may have designed plans and sought to stick to them unswervingly. But such an approach can turn plans into straightjackets, robbing people of their ability to adjust or make mid-course corrections. Such unblinking commitment can kill creativity. CEI's focus on innovation meant that stations were regularly forced to consider their goals and then, if necessary and appropriate, repeatedly adjust their efforts along the way—over and over and over again. The CEI work called on them to continually recalibrate their efforts to ensure that they were on the right trajectory to have the impact they set out to achieve. For leaders like Erik Jensen, the Director of Community Engagement at WSKG in Binghamton this was a dramatic shift in approach:

> Rich [Harwood] said something at the end of [a] workspace that resonated with me. "You need to have the plans, they're important to have and keep in place. But understand, this project is the business of innovation, and as you're innovating, it's that constant ability to reshape that plan as you're working, and the flexibility and the willingness to do that is really critical to this work."

For CEI, innovation is a way of thinking about one's work. Recall the comment of Kimberlie Kranich at Illinois Public

Media, who spoke of her work as a personal calling. Like so many public innovators, she also saw her work as highly strategic. So when she talks about CEI, and the innovation it sparked, she says:

> *The Harwood Institute is introspective. It's all about change, it's all about growth. But it's also about being strategic. So it's like you're being given permission to innovate with a network of people where it's safe to try this stuff.*

Each station came to CEI with plans it wanted to expand upon, plans it thought would create leverage in its community. But at its heart, CEI was not about individual projects. CEI was about an orientation, a posture, an attitude, a practice of creating and innovating in order to build the civic health of the community and deepen the station's local relevance. Amy Shaw in St. Louis, summed up the difference between a traditional project-based approach and one built around innovation very simply. "We tended to see things as projects. This is more than a project. This is how we're thinking about us."

CHAPTER 5

THEN,
LISTEN

A big part of what we learned is the value of stepping way back and saying, "I need to understand this community at its most basic level. I need to understand what makes the community tick, how communication happens, what the issues are. I need to understand these things in order to make a contribution, and I can't make assumptions about any of that."

BRENDA BARNES
GENERAL MANAGER
KUSC, LOS ANGELES

N O MATTER HOW COMPELLING the idea of turning outward may be, reorientation without new practices is
destined to have little impact. Without new practices,
people quickly revert to old ways of operating. So, then, how can
individuals and organizations begin to build the new practices
that support an outward turn?

One of the most critical steps for any group, including
public broadcasters, is one that takes them through the station's
front doors and out into the community. Recall that "knowing
your community" was one of Harwood's Four Building Blocks of
Turning Outward (see pages 14-16). To build that deeper understanding, the broadcasters needed to go into the community and
engage with people in a fundamentally different way than they
previously had done.

Some years ago, the Harwood Institute identified what we call
the "7 Public Knowledge Keys," critical guideposts for anyone seeking to make decisions about public work. This *public* knowledge
exists in direct contrast to expert knowledge—the kinds of data
and trend reports that make up the bulk of the information most
organizations collect and use when seeking to understand their
community. When we asked CEI broadcasters how well they knew
their community, like many individuals and organizations we've
worked with, they told us about their reams of data, marketing
trends, audience numbers, and demographic analyses.

To be clear, expert data are invaluable and necessary to good
decision making. But these data can never tell any of us how
people in the community talk about and experience the key
issues in their lives, or how those issues cluster together into webs
of concerns that capture and reflect what people value most. It
is not possible to know people's aspirations or the language and

Harwood 7 Public Knowledge Keys

The 7 Public Knowledge Keys come from 20 years of research into communities. They are essential for deeply understanding a community so you can take action in a way that is relevant and significant. The knowledge keys are:

• *Issues of concern:* the concerns, challenges, and issues that people talk about, and how they define them; the tensions they wrestle with

• *Aspirations:* aspirations people hold for their community and their future

• *Sense of place:* the history of people, places, and issues of concern; development and evolution of these over time; the look and feel of the community

• *Sources:* people in the community who are considered authentic, credible, and trusted, about the community or a topic; beyond "officials"

• *People:* what's valuable to people in their community heritage, sports, stories; the language used and norms

• *Civic places:* where people get together (offline, online, etc.) and where they can be engaged

• *Stereotypes to watch:* preconceived notions or professional biases you or others have about the community or topic you are exploring

phrases they use to reflect the meaning in their lives from a survey or an Arbitron report. And without a deep understanding of the community, it can be difficult (if not, at times, impossible) to figure out how to calibrate one's work so that it is relevant and significant to people. So, while both kinds of knowledge—expert and public—are important, it is essential to remember that expert knowledge can never substitute for public knowledge.

Mark Leonard at Illinois Public Media summed up the sentiments of many of his colleagues when he described the impact that public knowledge had upon his station:

We were predominantly inclined to go to experts, or our sources, our experts on our campus in the Champaign-Urbana community; but we actually wouldn't go and find the faces of the story, the people whose lives are affected. And we're finding that it's better storytelling, and that our presumptions about our knowledge of the community are probably shallow and ill-informed—or they have been in the past, and we're admitting it. We're working to make our understanding deeper and richer.

Brenda Barnes, General Manager for KUSC in Los Angeles, puts it this way:

A big part of what we learned from CEI is the value of stepping way back and saying, "I need to understand this community at its most basic level. I need to understand what makes the community tick, how communication happens, what the issues are. I need to understand these things in order to make a contribution, and I can't make assumptions about any of that."

Few stations began CEI with the tools and understanding to tap into this rich vein of public knowledge, nor did they have much experience with the kind of engagement that produces it. So we had the broadcasters hold a series of Community Conversations, a staple of Harwood efforts in communities, to begin to get them out into the community and to make concrete the potential of authentic engagement for their work.

Community Conversations are simple 90-minute conversations that take place with 12 to 15 community members discussing their aspirations for the community, what they see as the key issues of the community, and how they think the community might start to address these concerns. These conversations helped the stations build momentum—getting them out of their buildings and into the community—and put a different kind of knowledge on the table for innovating. We have seen a similar pattern repeated for nearly 20 years. When the Harwood Institute worked with newspapers throughout the 1990s, it wasn't until we were able to get editors and reporters out into the community—actually gaining public knowledge through Community Conversations and other means—that they were able to truly turn outward and begin the long journey of changing their mind-set and practices. Only then were they able to begin the process of deepening their relationship with the community. This is what happened with the public broadcasters.

For many of the broadcasters, engaging with the community was a daunting task initially. As Leonard said of public broadcasters, "We're all shy introverts. We don't really want to go out and touch the community. That seems to be somewhat of a shared personality trait. So it goes against our grain." Flo Rogers, General Manager of southern Nevada's KNPR, echoed this sentiment:

The radio universe is populated by people who would like to work in small rooms on their own. And that is not a way of working that is going to help us be a community institution. I was one of them. I would say to people, "I want to work in radio because I don't want to meet people. I want to work in a small room on my own with a microphone."

Hosting and leading Community Conversations understandably brought forth anxiety—a good deal of it. Their trepidation and discomfort—and, sometimes, even fear—are hard to overemphasize. We have seen such reactions in almost all of our initial

Community Conversations efforts with organizations, leaders, even with fellow citizens. Sometimes it's a fear of not knowing what to ask, or how to manage a conversation; others times it is because they believe they already have the knowledge they need, and what could people in the community ever offer?

But we also know that those organizations and leaders that are able to move quickly from reorientation to their first interactions with the community to applying what they learn, are far more likely to produce early and dramatic impact within the community. So, while the fear is understandable, we refused to let it derail the work.

Indeed, Community Conversations were a significant turning point for many public broadcasters. Even the stations that initially viewed these conversations with trepidation became dedicated converts. At one station, after weeks of planning and little action, the station's coach said to the broadcasters, "Don't be afraid, just do it!" When they did, the results were often surprising to them.

NPT, Nashville Public Television, is good example of the process. Its first Community Conversation was with long-time residents about the kind of community they wanted Nashville to be. For Kevin Crane, Vice President of Programming and Technology, the first conversation proved informative, even painless. The residents showed up and offered important insights. However, the next conversation loomed as a more daunting encounter. The participants were a group of new immigrants to the city. Would they show up? Would they be willing to talk? But, in the end, the second conversation was even more powerful and insightful than the first.

The main surprise for Crane and his team was that there was a great deal of overlap between the two groups' aspirations for Nashville. While tensions in the community were real, the two groups, rather than holding divergent views about what they wanted Nashville to become, revealed there was also a great deal of common ground from which to work. Based on this newly discovered understanding, the station began to identify ways to bring people together from the two groups. As we will see in Chapter VI, Crane's work in the community not only transformed NPT's CEI initiative but, more essentially, the way the station now thinks about and produces all documentaries. Reflecting on his CEI experience, he said:

> I think back to a year ago when we first started CEI, and I didn't really get it. I was willing to give it a try.... [But] the benefits of actually sitting down with a group of people from the community, and a diverse group of people, and just talking to them about how they feel has been incredible. And one direct benefit that I can see when you come out from behind the station and you actually do the research, you learn things that you just wouldn't expect.

Like Crane and many of his colleagues, Mark Leonard also was initially uncertain about holding Community Conversations. But for Leonard those first few steps in getting out into the community built a momentum and sense of possibility and focus that have carried the work forward since. This is how he sees the change:

> At the beginning of the summer, we were supposed to start out with some Community Conversations and that felt like a daunting task—felt like a lot of work. We were uncertain; our confidence wasn't high about doing it. I think the other stations felt the same way. But after that, I think it begins to be like running or an exercise program. The start of it is really hard, but once we got the first

one under our belt and the second one under our belt, it became
easier—they became more spontaneous. Then I started longing for
them. They were no longer hard work, they were no longer some-
thing that you dreaded or that was an obligation. You were anxious
to hear the next conversation, anxious to be surprised by the next
breakthrough. I wanted to know who was going to show up, what
perspectives were they going to bring.

Another example: wtip, the small, public radio station serving
Grand Marais at the tip of the Minnesota arrowhead, hesitated
before starting its Community Conversations, worrying whether
it would find a warm welcome in the community, as the community had been undergoing dramatic changes in recent years.
New and long-time residents had become increasingly resentful of
one another. These tensions existed just beneath the surface, and
everyone was only too happy to keep them there. So how would
the community react to its public broadcasting station asking people to talk for 90 minutes about the kind of community
they wanted?

After just one conversation, wtip found that not only was such
a discussion eagerly embraced but that even in a town as small as
Grand Marais, the Community Conversations brought forward
ideas, issues, and aspirations that staff said they would never have
heard any other way. What started with reticence and uncertainty
soon became one of the most critical changes for the small station.
As Deb Benedict, the General Manager and one of only two full-
time staff, said:

As a small, rural, volunteer-based community station, I felt
we were more engaged with our community to begin with than

some of my cohorts were with theirs. However, the Community Conversations were absolutely the best. I learned more about our community members, their needs, desires, issues, and goals and the diversity within the community than I thought I would. And as hard as it was to kick off the Conversations, they were wonderful. We gathered folks from all different groups in the community.... We conducted probably 16 different Community Conversations over a period of 6 months. [We asked] the question, "What kind of community do you want?" It was just phenomenal.... It was just real heartwarming to realize that we were providing hopefully the start of a different sort of dialogue in our community. I didn't really know what to expect. When we started the Community Engagement Initiative and were given all the tools, and the terms, and the charts, my head was spinning. I didn't really know how to begin, but frankly, I was kind of amazed. Be it any of the groups—locals not having experienced the bigger world, or groups that have experienced the bigger world and chose to live here—the reaction was real similar. It got people thinking about "Wow, what do we want for our community? And how is our community, and how can it be different? And what can we do to change that?"

In Grand Marais, these conversations opened up new spaces within the community for people to talk together about topics that were rarely addressed. As a result, the conversations led the station to rethink its role in the community and its potential to play a new role in strengthening the community's civic health. Now, Community Conversations have become the lynchpin of the station's work, and the engine for new ways for WTIP to help the community re-create itself.

By the end of CEI, station leaders talked about gaining a deeper understanding of the community as one of the most powerful outcomes from their work. Holding this rich sense of the community paid enormous dividends, as stations found themselves better able to understand their communities and the productive role they could play in them.

CHAPTER 6

OCCUPYING
A NEW SPACE

It's about aspiring to be something different than what we were in the past when we just pushed out stuff and hoped people liked it, used it. I think it's creating this new role for us as public media, and a place we can hold in our communities. The conversations that we can be a part of and help bring to life, it's serving a different purpose. And it's using the power of the medium that we exist in for a higher purpose.... I think it's just envisioning a new role for us as an organization, and how we can be an essential part of a community. We are rewriting the book of what we can be as public institutions that serve our community.

JOHN KING
GENERAL MANAGER
VERMONT PUBLIC TELEVISION

W E BEGAN CEI CONFIDENT that the 12 stations—indeed, all public broadcasters—could play a more vital role in building the civic health of their communities and be more locally significant. This shift, even transformation, played out as the stations turned outward and came to know their communities. Stations began to see their relationship to community differently, sometimes dramatically so. One of Maryland Public Television's project memos reflected the station's changing role in the community: "We feel we are making real progress towards redefining our roles as provocateur, public innovator, convenor, storyteller, catalyst, and connector—quite different from that of a mere television station or PBS pass-through."

At the start of CEI, many stations viewed their on-air content and programs as their primary asset. After all, these are broadcasters. But through CEI, they discovered the incredible array of resources and assets they could leverage to strengthen the health of the community. What's more, many of these assets had little to do specifically with broadcasting, and everything to do with how the station envisioned its relationship with the community. Flo Rogers at KNPR in Las Vegas, captured this change when she said:

> The most significant thing to come out of this for us was how we think of ourselves in relation to the communities we serve. I believe we've really underestimated one of our greatest strengths in public broadcasting and that is that we can play a true leadership role in our communities. The Community Engagement Initiative helped us uncover the potential of that role here in Southern Nevada.

Midway through CEI, we asked the stations to list the roles they saw themselves playing within the community, and they identified options many of which might have seemed foreign or wayward at the start. These roles included:

- *Connector*
- *Convenor*
- *Partner/promoter*
- *Capacity builder*
- *Storyteller*
- *Candid friend to the community*
- *Resource*
- *Catalyst*
- *Archivist of shared history*
- *Conduit for agents of change*
- *Trusted partner providing pathways to understanding*

What unlocked this floodgate of potential roles? For many of the stations, it was answering a single question that we put to them early in the initiative: What space do you occupy in the community? This question helped crystallize in a new way a station's relationship with the community. It served to pull together a variety of CEI threads—giving the stations a way to see the value of turning outward, their newly articulated aspirations, their growing understanding of the community, and their focus on creating community impact. Taken together, these themes were critical elements in helping them remember and recognize why we're here.

A *Part* of the Community

The answers to the "what space?" question reflected the dramatic shift stations had made since the start of CEI. Initially, most stations

saw themselves as operating at the center of their community—
that is, they spoke of the community in relationship to themselves.
This organization-first view was brought into sharp focus when we
asked the stations to draw a picture representing their communities and their work within them. For many, the station building sat
in the very center of the picture. Around the station, you might see
representations of partners, listeners, viewers, and donors, each and
all of whom interacted with the station but not necessarily with one
another. By and large, these groups orbited around the station. The
station was the "center of the universe."

In all fairness, these scenes were no different from those of
other groups we've asked to draw such pictures. For example,
when we asked local arts organizations to do this, they, too,
placed themselves at the center of the community. They, too, saw
the community only through their own organization's eyes. In
their perspective, they alone held knowledge about the arts, and
they alone were responsible for providing arts programs in the
community. They were the creators, distributors, and owners of
the arts. During the discussions about these drawings, the arts
groups soon discovered that they had separated themselves from
the very community they wished to be a part of.

After the CEI stations presented their pictures to one another,
we asked the broadcasters to reflect on them. Were communities
simply satellites orbiting the station? Would people in the community have placed the station at the center of the picture as well?
They quickly saw the problem. After some discussion, we asked
the broadcasters to revise their pictures, and this time their view
of the relationship between station and community looked quite
different. The pictures now featured an interwoven community
(or the potential for such). Now, stations were connecting people

to one another—not simply to the station itself. Now, partners played a major role helping stations connect with different communities, creating new spaces for conversation, and enabling people to take action with others. Taken as a whole, the new drawings suggested a new alignment for the stations: they had an essential role to play, but they were not the center of the community. This time the community was the focal point.

Finding the Right Fit

The question, what space do you occupy?, fundamentally asked stations to think about how they fit within the community. The notion of "fit" is radically different from assuming that one is at the center. It suggests that the community already exists and that the station is *part of* it rather than operating *apart from* it. It means that the station must come to understand where it sits in relationship to others—where it fits with others—rather than simply to impose itself. Instead of envisioning the community in relation to the station, now they described their work in distinctly more public terms. They were in relationship with the community.

An incredible energy was unleashed once people saw their station in this way. For many CEI leaders the realization of just how inwardly focused they and their colleagues had become was revealing, even jolting. As Joe Krushinsky at Maryland Public Television, commented:

> *We sometimes, and probably more often than we'd care to admit throughout our history, forgot—the community is what this is all about. And so every once in a while we get a certain hubris about*

"knowing what the community wants and knowing how to make good public media content," and it all becomes very insular and in-house thinking.

The tide began to turn in response to the "what space?" question, and stations began writing statements that offered a new view of their role in the community. Here are some examples:

• *We connect organizations to each other to bring music opportunities to the community. To better connect community members through music.*

• *We strengthen civic health and build better lives.*

• *We create a web of interconnected networks and pathways in the communities we serve for the greater good.*

• *We are creating an online environment that connects the community and creates a safe space for discussion.*

• *We improve communities through public service media.*

For Vermont Public Television, the "what space?" question provided a pivotal turning point in the station's journey. As one leader shared with us:

There is no shortage of what we would like to be doing, but now more than ever it is imperative that we look at the scope of our organization and the space we hope to occupy in our communities, and take the necessary steps to ensure we are a significant and relevant community resource.

The notion of "what space?" gained traction within CEI stations because it connected to the participants' aspirations for public broadcasting. As we saw earlier, focusing on aspirations helped stations create the momentum, energy, and focus to support turning outward. Station staff found that the potential for their station to play new roles within the community resonated deeply—genuinely—with their aspirations for the work. As Mark Leonard at Illinois Public Media observed:

[We are] beginning to see genuine change in our staff and how they are viewing their roles and the role of the organization. There is a genuine excitement that seems to be coming out of many of the staff members.... I think it gives purpose to their work; it gives meaning to their work. They didn't know they missed it, or that they needed it, or that it was something that was a distant memory that is rekindled by thinking of your community and your relationship to it in different ways. It's a pleasurable experience.

Before CEI, the stations often talked about their programming as their primary connection to the community. They would create programs, air them, and oftentimes undertake outreach efforts in service of them. But as they came to consider the space they sought to occupy, some stations literally began moving into the community. For Robin Pressman, Program Director at KRCB in Sonoma County, California, this reorientation meant finding new ways of working. "[We are] going beyond broadcast, bringing the community into the project. We're breaking down the walls of KRCB and moving into a public space."

Other stations similarly saw themselves becoming part of the
web of the community. At KUSC in Los Angeles, Brenda Barnes was
thrilled by how the community responded to her station's efforts to
become more of a part of the community:

We really went from being an organization outside the commu-
nity, sort of a carpetbagger, to being an organization that's part
of the arts community. One of the most powerful moments for
us came at one of our last meetings, when one of the people who
works for the Palm Springs Arts Museum stood up and said, "You
know what, I can't begin to tell you how much it means that you're
coming here, you're meeting us, you care about our community,
you want to try to help us move the arts community forward. It
really means a huge amount." So, for them to recognize us as a
part of the arts community and an important contributor to the
arts community really told us that our efforts were paying off.

With this experience, KUSC felt that it had finally arrived—that
is, that it was finally a part of the larger community. As one staff
member put it, "We are suddenly a viable part of the community.
We are actually a leader."

For some stations, like WPBT in Miami, the shift to being a
part of the community entailed moving from a technology-based
focus to a community focus. WPBT came to CEI intent on building
uVu, a YouTube-like platform for posting and sharing videos. But
over time, the station recognized that its goal shouldn't simply
be to build a technology platform for hosting content. Rather, it
could and should work to build community through technology.
Refocusing its efforts on the community has dramatically altered
what WPBT does, as Neal Hecker explains: "We really have seen

community become the pinnacle of everything. All our work focuses on what that means… the idea of serving community is foremost in everything we plan and do now."

For other stations, the shift meant seeing themselves becoming invaluable resources for the community. Erik Jensen, the Director of Community Engagement for wskg in Binghamton, describes his vision for what the station could be:

Ultimately, the role I would like to see us strive for is not just sort of a broadcaster. Instead, I think as people struggle with issues that they think of public broadcasting as a potential resource in regards to helping them address the issues—that more people begin to think of public broadcasting as one of a number of important institutions in their area that help them address and solve problems.

Jensen also told us of his surprise in hearing his colleagues talk about the station's new orientation with fervor and energy. Here's how he paraphrased what they told him: "This is the type of thing I've always wanted to be able to do more of, but didn't feel like I had the leeway, or there wasn't the authority or the importance in the organization to make this stuff happen." He went on to report that "some people that have said that that's the role they felt public broadcasting should have been playing anyway…. It is sort of liberating for them."

For wtip in Grand Marais, when the Community Conversations brought forward community issues that were rarely acknowledged much less discussed, the broadcasters realized they could be more than just broadcasters—that by being a convenor and by creating spaces for conversations, they could have a profound community impact. In the station's final cei memo, it wrote:

As we look forward, we are embracing our role in the community. We recognize that we have an ability to help initiate positive change through discussion, connection, and information sharing. We have become a significant local organization, important to and deeply involved in the civic life of our community.

One of the most direct statements of how a station changed after exploring its space and fit in the community, comes from KRCB in Sonoma County. After participating in CEI the station now describes its goals as follows: "Attempting to build a healthier community which has the capacity to identify and work on the challenges of the future." Rather than focus on building the station's brand, or driving up the size of the audience, or even raising additional dollars, the station is focused outward, working to build a healthier community and not simply a healthier station, and to build the community's capacity and not solely its own capacity. Here's how Nancy Dobbs, the station's general manager, captured the new essence of the station's role: "Our core mission is to use telecommunications resources to strengthen community involvement and community discourse. We are bringing people back into the community square."

CHAPTER 7

NEW PROGRAMMING, NEW PARTNERS, NEW ONLINE SPACES

I hate to throw around bravery, but I think we're brave enough to say this is what people are talking about. It's a version of saying, "What's relevant to people?" and that's what we need to be talking about. We weren't hearing what was relevant five years ago. We were deciding what was relevant five years ago.

NEAL HECKER
VICE PRESIDENT FOR PROGRAMMING
WBPT, MIAMI

T URNING OUTWARD HELPED MANY CEI stations transform both how they view their relationship with the community and how the community sees them. By turning outward and seeking impact, the stations began sending new signals to the community and other public broadcasters about the potential role for public broadcasting in community life. This chapter details some examples. By themselves, none of these examples can adequately capture the energy and trajectory of the change that emerged from each station, or across the stations. But taken together they show the power of turning outward. And they reflect a growing case for public broadcasters as to why we're here.

A Philosophical Shift in Programming

Through the Community Conversations, many stations found that their existing on-air programs, while well produced and often well received, did not adequately reflect people's concerns, their aspirations, or the tensions within their communities. Instead of trying to fix this by simply changing the topic on a single show, CEI stations took bolder and more intentional actions. This realization led, as one broadcaster said, to "a philosophical shift" in how the stations think about and do programming. Simply put, stations' new approach to programming sent new signals to listeners and viewers.

For our first example of such a "philosophical shift," we take another look at the tension in the small community served by WTIP in northern Minnesota. WTIP's Community Conversations helped the station uncover "taboo" community issues, which included issues around public schooling, land use and the environment, the changing economy, and the stress that comes with the influx of new residents. Once these issues surfaced, the WTIP staff, through its involvement in CEI, came to believe that the station could and should step forward to play a role in holding a mirror up to people so they could see these issues, engage with them, and hear one another. For the station, this wasn't a burden but a golden opportunity to help people reknit the fabric of the community and see and hear one another in a fundamentally different way.

Station staff also realized that to do it right, they would need to create an entirely new monthly program dedicated to such issues, which came to be called *First Thursday*. In effect, the program sent a new signal about the role and potential of the station and about the kind of conversations that were possible in Grand Marais. General Manager Deb Benedict described the program this way: "It got people thinking about 'Wow, what do we want for our community? And how is our community, and how can it be different? And what can we do to change that?'"

We noted earlier that Community Conversations became a lynchpin for the stations' work. This is seen clearly with *First Thursday*. New topics and ideas for *First Thursday* came directly from ongoing Community Conversations, which continue to this day. The program seeks to spark the same kind of in-depth, nuanced conversations that take place in the Community Conversations, and in turn hopes to spark even broader and deeper conversations throughout the community. One of the explicit goals of *First Thursday* is for people to see that they can talk openly, productively, and even civilly about tough issues. Indeed, the station recognized that beyond good programming they could help create norms that are productive for community discussion. It is one thing to produce a program that influences what people talk about, but WTIP was doing more than that—*First Thursday* helped influence both *what* people talked about and *how* they talked with one another.

So, when the station heard about the rising tension between public school and charter school advocates, they brought together the two officials who had been publicly clashing but who, even in the small town of Grand Marais, had never met before. Rather than simply seek to exploit the easy hot-button issues, *First Thursday* focused the conversation on the community's aspirations and the future of education in the area ... and something surprising happened along the way. In the course of the program, while on-air, the two leaders made a public pledge to begin meeting with one another. And they have done just that. As the comment we quoted earlier from Deb Benedict says, "It was real heartwarming to realize that we were providing hopefully the start of a different sort of dialogue in our community."

Recognizing the hunger within the community to engage, WTIP started to hold Community Conversations after their *First Thursday* programs so people could continue the on-air conversation. Through a combination of on- and off-air resources, WTIP has successfully opened up new spaces in the community where people can talk through tough public issues. Benedict explains that in just a short period of time there have been noticeable differences in the community:

There has been a shift in our community as far as folks learning to try and understand each other.... We're trying to get people to know each other so they might not have ... misunderstandings about others, as our community goes forward in order to solve common problems. We're really seeing more people attend public meetings to get involved with the city or the county.... Especially right now, dealing with energy issues, we're seeing more people engaged, more people attending meetings, and more people involved with the whole seeking-of-information process on what people want. I think we believe that it has a lot to do with creating an atmosphere of less hostility and more understanding among people. We're trying to make our community a safer place for people to come out and voice their opinions.

Such shifts occurred in many other stations.

In Nashville, NPT came to CEI with a focus on bolstering its Local Services Initiative documentary series, *Next Door Neighbors: Immigrants and Refugees.* The initial plans called for producers to craft four documentaries, each on a different immigrant group, and then to pursue traditional community outreach activities. By the time the station was ready to work on the documentaries, it had incorporated the idea of Community Conversations into its operations. The first of the Community Conversations was to engage the Kurdish community, and it utterly changed the station's approach to the making of documentaries. Broadly, the Conversations showed the station's producers that their understanding of the Kurdish community barely skimmed the surface. More specifically, it was at this Community Conversation that the producers first heard of a key figure in the Kurdish community, a local used car salesman whose dealership serves as an afternoon gathering place for Kurdish immigrants. These immigrants found the car dealership a natural place to gather for conversation, familiar foods, and access to a key resource—cars!

No list of "official leaders" would have yielded this gentleman's name. But when producers spoke with him and then with others in the community, they came to know the Kurdish community in a fundamentally different way. As a result, they sought out different sources than they originally had intended to contact and, to engage the community, they connected with different partners. Ultimately, this led them to reframe their whole documentary and subsequent engagement efforts. Starting with people in the community rather than with issue experts meant an approach that was built from the ground up.

Taking a new approach to working with the Kurdish community helped the station produce a stronger documentary, but, even more to the point, it changed the station's relationship with the Kurdish community. According to Kevin Crane, NPT's Vice President of Programming and Technology, the station is now seen as more relevant and significant:

> *In general, I would say that people five years ago thought of NPT as somewhat inaccessible—and certainly within the Kurdish community. Well, they don't think of us as inaccessible at all now. The Kurdish community was just head over heels about being asked and being featured. One of the people who was in the doc said, "What have we done to make this wonderful thing happen in our community, where people are actually asking us 'What's it like to live here, and who are you, and where did you come from?'" That was one of the best things that could've happened in the community.*

For each of the three subsequent documentaries, NPT again started with Community Conversations. "Talking" to the community was no longer a luxury or a task just for the outreach department—it was now a critical part of how the station created content. Crane says, "[I] can't imagine doing a documentary without first doing Community Conversations." According to him, "Outreach was something the outreach department used to do. Now the production people don't see it that way." The success of the *Next Door Neighbors* series has been a catalyst for altering the way NPT thinks about its production process and its work with the community. And now this approach, using Harwood ideas and frameworks, is being spread by NPT throughout the public broadcasting system.

Here's another example. In southern Nevada, KNPR's signature program *State of Nevada* was, by all traditional measures, a great success. The two-hour daily radio show covered national news stories and intriguing local issues with obvious skill and craft. But, as KNPR turned outward, it discovered just how deeply isolated and disconnected people in the region felt from one another. It discovered that a sense of place was missing from the community—and that *State of Nevada*'s coverage of national issues, while important, wasn't addressing these concerns.

So, KNPR made the tough decision to restructure *State of Nevada*. Think about this decision. KNPR wasn't using what it learned about the local community to tweak a struggling program or tinker with its programming at the margins. KNPR was so focused on creating community impact that it was willing to use what it had learned to fundamentally reshape its most prominent and most successful program.

The goal: to focus more intently on locally relevant issues and help foster people's connection to one another. This meant the show would have to trade-off covering "hot" stories in favor of a clearer focus on daily life and issues in southern Nevada. By changing its signature program, KNPR was sending a signal to the staff and the broader community that the station's outward turn was not just cosmetic. The station was transforming itself.

The staff was willing to accept that this new approach might have community impact, but would it find an audience? The results spoke for themselves. According to one KNPR report:

> *Our audience for this one program [State of Nevada] has grown more than 20 percent in the last year. CEI has helped us keep "on message" as a public affairs broadcast that is about our community, our issues, our challenges, people finding solutions and helping us understand the culture, economics, and politics of our region.*

Many months later, KNPR continues to innovate and transform *State of Nevada* by bringing in a new host and doubling its efforts to focus on issues that matter to people locally.

On the other side of the country, WSKG in Binghamton serves a community that could hardly be more different than KNPR's Las Vegas. The Binghamton area has long been down-and-out and, some say, held hostage to the ingrained narrative of abandonment, decay, and the inability to chart a different course than the one that plagues so many old manufacturing communities. For years, WSKG produced programs celebrating Binghamton's glorious but long-passed industrial history or lamenting its current and seemingly intractable problems. Both the station and the community had become stuck in this rut.

As part of its work with CEI, the station shifted how it views the community and its relationship to it. One step has been to focus on people's positive efforts in the community, but not in the usual public relations way of being a community booster or an uncritical cheerleader. WSKG is now leading the charge to reengage and reconnect people with the community's future squarely in view. WSKG developed *Chasing Change*, a series of "interstitials"— short television pieces—that spotlight emerging stories of hope and impact from within the community. WSKG also launched *Community Conversation*, a radio program targeted at helping engage people with each other around key issues that emerged from the Community Conversations held by the station. This program expands the reach of the Conversations and sends new signals to the community about the possibility for moving forward and about the potential roles that people can play in taking action to change the story of Binghamton.

Vermont Public Television is also sending out new signals from its flagship public affairs program, *Public Square*. The station made the difficult choice to refocus the program by framing issues in *public* ways—that is, based on public knowledge that the station gathers—rather than framing it predominantly on a policy- or expert-knowledge perspective. In addition, the station has made a commitment to stick with individual issues over time. This is a significant change from highlighting "the issue of the month" and then moving to the next topic. This change may sound easy or obvious, but was neither; it required the station to rethink its role in the community and the state of Vermont.

WPBT in Miami is another station that stepped forward to create programming to tackle issues that emerged from its Community Conversations and engagement efforts. Even amid tough financial times, WPBT launched *Pulse*, a new Caribbean public affairs program that is the result of Conversations and new partnerships the station formed through CEI. This is another example of a station moving in a direction that was only discovered by turning outward. Neal Hecker, Vice President for

Programming, describes the challenge of creating *Pulse* and the change in approach that the show embodies:

> *We've launched a Caribbean public affairs program [Pulse] that's dealing with some issues we've just never dealt with on air. Internally, it's hard to carve time out of schedules to do this because everybody now is doing two or three jobs. But we saw getting involved … as a priority for what we do here. It was something we felt was missing from what we do.… Even out of the gate, the first topic was on this homophobic Jamaican dance hall music. I've got to tell you that is not a subject we would've tackled on a public affairs show three years ago.*

We asked Hecker why a topic like "homophobic Jamaican dance hall music" was something that the station was willing to tackle now. He explained that the connection to the community the station had developed through CEI gave them more confidence:

> *Well, I hate to throw around bravery, but I think we're brave enough to say this is what people are talking about. This [the program on the dance hall music] is how we need to respond. It's a version of saying, "What's relevant to people?" and that's what we need to be talking about. We weren't hearing what was relevant five years ago. We were deciding what was relevant five years ago.*

Each of these examples demonstrates how turning outward fundamentally altered the way stations thought about and crafted their most obvious asset—their programs. We should note, too, that making these changes sometimes meant facing fierce resistance from within the stations. For years, staff alone determined what was relevant and what was worthy of being produced, oftentimes seeing the community merely as recipients or audience for those programs. As Hecker said, "We weren't *hearing* what was relevant five years ago. We were *deciding* what was relevant five years ago." But through CEI, stations altered that relationship—placing community at the heart of the production process.

New Partnerships and Networks

With the community in clearer view, and a determined focus on impact, the CEI stations started to change how and with whom they partnered. In many cases, this led them to alter, even abandon, long-standing relationships—an enormously difficult shift for any organization to make. Over the years, we've found that such shifts occur and take root only when a deep sense of purpose exists. These more intentional partnerships helped build new networks in the community, reweave the very fabric of community, and enable people to shape their own future and that of their community.

In St. Louis, KETC's *Facing the Mortgage Crisis* is an example of the power of reshaping how a station partners with others. The effort not only represented a major shift in programming—an important change—but it also fundamentally reshaped how KETC sees the space it occupies and how it works within the community. The initiative began in response to the surge of foreclosures that hit St. Louis and other communities like a tidal wave. Thus the simple but audacious goal of this new effort: connect St. Louis residents to organizations and resources that would help them deal with the mortgage foreclosures crisis and related financial concerns.

In the past, KETC's response to a mortgage crisis might have been to produce a solid television program on the problem and work to build audience via traditional outreach activities. This time the station took a different path. Rather than try to play the role of a financial expert, which it might have done in the past, KETC instead sought to connect people to other groups in the community with that financial expertise. The change in the underlying assumption is noteworthy. KETC recognized that it didn't need to "own" or even deliver expert or technical resources themselves. They could best serve the people of St. Louis by being a facilitator and connecting people directly to those community resources.

So, the station brought together a core group of 25 local groups and organizations, from United Way of Greater St. Louis and the St. Louis Public Library to NeighborWorks America, the Urban League, and Catholic Charities. Pulling these groups together helped create a new and needed network in the community.

For a station that has turned outward, it makes sense to connect people to the resources they need, even when it means connecting them to *other* nonprofits and groups. In this way, the objective for the station was not simply to aggregate an audience or drive up the number of hits on their Web site. People in the community were hurting, and the station sought to get out the basic information people needed to stay in their homes and help them make sense of the unprecedented changes in the economy. Our own experience working with communities tells us that, sadly, the station's chosen path here is not the norm among community groups. Even the most well-intentioned groups find themselves trying to soak up as much public attention as possible, and keep valuable relationships with community members to themselves rather than directing people elsewhere.

Did KETC's efforts actually have a community impact? According to a University of Wisconsin evaluation, *Facing the Mortgage Crisis* made a measurable community wide increase in the interactions of neighbors around these issues. There was a 27.7 percent increase in the sharing of mortgage crisis information and personal concerns among St. Louis residents who watched the program. Additionally, 35.9 percent more people who watched the program said they were likely to share information about resources—like the United Way's 2-1-1 helpline or the mortgage crisis Web site—than those who did not see the program. KETC's approach clearly helped people become their own problem solvers.

Did anyone notice KETC's good work? Again, the answer is yes. KETC experienced what each of the other CEI stations found—that turning outward strengthened the station's sustainability. According to the University of Wisconsin evaluation, *Facing the Mortgage Crisis* increased by 22.6 percent the likelihood of people supporting KETC.

In Nevada, KNPR's award-winning *Community Connections* program had for years identified and highlighted local nonprofit groups doing good work in the community. The effort, like *State of Nevada*, was already a huge success before CEI. Nonetheless, as KNPR began to rethink and reshape its relationship with the community, for the first time it reached out to nonprofit leaders to discuss how to better leverage the program to produce a deeper community impact.

What station leaders heard surprised them. The nonprofit leaders, after learning about the ideas behind CEI, argued that instead of solely finding and highlighting worthy nonprofits, the station should continue to identify community aspirations and challenges, and then, informed by that public knowledge, highlight those local nonprofits that specifically addressed issues salient to the community. So, rather than starting by identifying the nonprofit groups to feature—some of which were now sitting around the table with KNPR—*Community Connections* would leverage KNPR's engagement efforts to identify the issues *people* were actually wrestling with and *then* find the nonprofits that best enabled people to act on their own concerns and aspirations for their communities. Changing *Community Connections* sent a clear signal to its nonprofit partners about the new space that KNPR sought to occupy.

It was a signal to one of its financial supporters as well. Around the time that KNPR reshaped *Community Connections*, Wells Fargo Bank cut back its philanthropic support to every one of its Las Vegas grantees—that is, except for KNPR. We told this story earlier when discussing the financial potential of this work, but it is worth repeating. Wells Fargo recognized the station's growing community impact and the potential of its new approach to *Community Connections*, so not only was KNPR not cut, it received an increase.

Meanwhile, in the previous five years of producing *Community Connections*, KNPR had invested a great deal of energy and time in collecting, cataloguing, and presenting information about the region's most effective nonprofits. You might expect KNPR would focus on leveraging this resource to become *the* site for learning about local nonprofits. But that's not what KNPR did, not by a long shot.

Rather than trying to own that information, General Manager Flo Rogers looked for ways to give it away and ensure that more people in southern Nevada had the opportunity to identify resources to help them find their way into public life or access needed social services. This goal led her to reach out to an unlikely partner—a cluster of commercial radio stations. Rogers explains the partnership this way:

> *This is something that came directly out of* CEI. *We have a cluster of radio stations called the Lotus Broadcast Group. They have Spanish language and hard rock. They have 400,000 listeners that don't listen to us. The overlap with us is nothing, it's really insignificant. Instead of telling people to go to individual station Web sites, the group created one site called WeAreLasVegas. com. They don't say, "Go to Hard Rock 97.com," they say, "Go to WeAreLasVegas.com." They're looking at their cluster of stations as a conglomeration of audiences. It doesn't matter if you listen to hard rock or whatever, you probably love sports, you might be looking for a community activity… and so all of those Web sites feed into the same site. And we said, "Why don't you let us provide the community piece through* Community Connections *because we make it our business to evaluate the organizations and ask them for certain kinds of information before we put them on our list of 100 or so some pages that we maintain."*

When she explained this to her board, the board members were initially incredulous. After all, here Rogers was giving a group of commercial stations access to information that the station had collected over five years, and KNPR now would no longer be the only source for this knowledge. Here's how she describes the conversation:

They would say, "Why are you giving that work away? You've worked for five years to maintain this database of really great nonprofits and keep it up-to-date. Why would you give that away?" And my answer is, "There are 400,000 people who listen to those radio stations. They don't listen to us. Don't we have a responsibility to ensure that they have credible information about the nonprofits operating in town? Don't the people out there that don't listen to us, don't they want to help the community as much as our listeners do? Our listeners don't have the franchise on caring about this place."

Turning outward led Rogers to come to a fundamentally different conclusion. As she says, "We don't own this information. This is not information that I have the ability to be exclusive about. The 100 nonprofits on our list, I don't own the ability to decide where that information goes." That's a conclusion that comes from turning outward and focusing on community impact.

KNPR's work with the Lotus Broadcasting Group is just one of several examples of the station strategically seeking partnerships that have enabled it to create community impact. Ahead of the 2008 Democratic Presidential Primary, KNPR partnered with yet another commercial radio station that primarily reaches the African American community; by teaming up, the two stations were able to dramatically expand the number of people with access to information about the issues facing southern Nevada. Partnering with a commercial station, particularly one that had little overlap with KNPR's traditional public broadcasting audience would simply not have made sense to the staff at KNPR before CEI.

As stations turn outward, they often face hard choices and judgments about whether existing partners can help them create the kind of impact they seek. They often find they need new or different partners. Over the course of their work with CEI, many stations realized that their long-time partners no longer fit the bill given the station's new approach. The question we persistently asked the stations was, "Who do you want to run with?" That is, given scarce resources, whom do you truly need in order to create the greatest impact? Often stations discovered that their traditional allies were disconnected from the community and unwilling to engage in ways that put the community at the center of their efforts.

NPT, in Nashville, was one station that faced this tough choice. The grant that funded NPT's *Next Door Neighbors* documentary series specifically identified Vanderbilt University as the host for one of NPT's post-broadcast outreach forums with local immigrants. Vanderbilt had long been one of the station's strongest and most reliable partners; and it is one of the nation's premier higher education institutions. So it only made sense that prior to CEI, the two organizations agreed to partner on this key effort. However, as the station turned outward and engaged with immigrants in the community, it realized that Vanderbilt alone could not help the station reach its goals. The university had few deep connections within the local immigrant community, and few immigrants ever walked onto the hallowed university campus. But there it was right in the grant—after it aired the documentary, NPT had to have a group of immigrants come to Vanderbilt to talk about the program.

To change the location meant talking to NPT's funder and reshaping the grant—something few organizations would relish, especially in tough economic times. But NPT decided that it had a responsibility to use what it learned from CEI, and so it went back to the funder and renegotiated the agreement. In the process, the station found that to broaden its reach in the community, it would have to recruit a different set of partners. Rather than work solely with Vanderbilt, NPT reached out to groups that were committed to extending conversations throughout the community—and had deeper ties in their communities than did Vanderbilt.

Of course, if you've ever cultivated new partners, you know that it is not always a comfortable or an easy process. For instance, NPT found that many of the groups most interested in holding the Community Conversations also held strong advocacy agendas. What's more, the station learned that to create real impact in the community, it often had to consider working with groups other than the "usual suspects." All this forced the station to establish clear parameters for how the partnerships would work and what activities would fit with the space the station was trying to occupy.

The key lesson that NPT has taken from this work is the importance of focusing first on the community impact it sought to create, and then trying to align with the right partners.

Online Spaces as Community Spaces

Like many organizations, CEI stations initially saw their Web sites as places to celebrate, archive, support, and promote their own efforts. These sites functioned essentially as billboards for the station. But as the stations sought to create community impact, they came to see their sites as a key asset with greater community potential. Several of the stations restructured their sites to make them community hubs or portals—a resource for connecting people to one another rather than as a billboard for the station. These new portals place the community, and not the station, at the center.

The online sites of KNPR in Nevada and Vermont Public Television are strong examples of the change. Both stations have been working to transform their Web sites into community portals. These sites now enable listeners and viewers and others to connect with community groups, and with one another, to further explore and act on community concerns.

For KNPR's partners in particular, this change has had a dramatic impact. The station now connects more than 15,000 people a month to resources on partners' sites. As the changes to *State of Nevada* demonstrate, KNPR put a stake in the ground to create opportunities for Nevadans to return to community and public life. For General Manager Flo Rogers, then, the changes to the Web site make clear sense:

> *[We're] trying to invite people in, rather than simply being a companion site to the programming. And we are orienting our entire organization from the top down to an idea that our role in the community is to sort of own that space around the dialogue about who we are as a community and developing that sense of place and that sense of community.*

Earlier we described how WPBT in Miami transformed its uVu site from a station-focused platform into a community platform. When WPBT joined CEI it was seeking to develop uVu into an online space for sharing station-produced video and other content and to promote it through station outreach. In this model, the community remained largely a passive audience. But WPBT has been fundamentally transforming uVu into something quite different. Now the site is a space for communitywide engagement between and among groups and individuals who may never interact with WPBT. Previous content for the site was created in the station and shared, now content typically comes from the community. According to WPBT:

For uVu, we continue to try and create the space where conversation and discussions can take place and build in a safe environment for these conversations. The challenge here is in creating a trusted environment for listening to the community and ensuring that the stories we tell are in fact the stories that the community wants (needs) to hear. Where this dovetails with uVu is that the opportunity exists for the community to tell the story itself; there can be no greater authority than that.

The station is finding that changing its approach to uVu has shifted the way it relates to organizations and community partners. For instance, community partners such as Imagine Miami (a network of partner organizations, linking people with financial education, health-care information, public benefits, and educational and economic opportunities, and a long-time Harwood partner) have come to see uVu as "their" platform to broadcast and connect with the community. Imagine Miami now creates uVu videos to share its perspectives with other Miamians, to generate its own community discussions, and to spark local action.

The evolving nature of uVu has also changed the way WPBT chooses to cover local events. Before these recent changes, WPBT would scurry about trying to sort out requests to send overworked camera crews to shoot this or that event. Now, when local organizations contact the station about an event, WPBT offers to lend the groups simple digital video cameras to create and post their own videos to uVu. Such changes might have been unthinkable before.

These innovations have produced a huge impact on many of the organizations featured on uVu, and people in the community are taking notice. Recently, one organization head wrote the station that after uVu featured a forthcoming event called "A Day For Children," tens of thousands attended it, stating, "Have you any idea of how you have touched the lives of so many families and so many children in our community? Many of these children would never have had the opportunities they had this past Sunday."

In the past, such an event would have been too "small" to air, but by changing the way it works in the community, WPBT has created a platform for helping organizations and people connect with one another. By turning outward, WPBT was able to create a resource for the community and its partners and to establish new connections to groups it would never have worked with before.

CHAPTER 8

A NEW COMMUNITY RESOURCE

We're being invited to be at the table in dialogues where we've never been before. Suddenly we were seen as a player. They are looking to us to participate given our expertise in engagement and our stature as a trusted community institution.

MARK LEONARD
GENERAL MANAGER
ILLINOIS PUBLIC MEDIA

THE MORE CEI STATIONS turned outward the more they found other groups were eager to work with them; increasingly, they were being seen as a valuable community resource. Before CEI, stations had been a sought-after partner primarily because of their broadcast capabilities. Now that equation was changing, as the stations occupied a different space within the community and had new skills and new knowledge about the community.

More than Media

In Sonoma County, California, KRCB General Manager Nancy Dobbs found that her staff's expertise in Community Conversations helped reposition the station in the eyes of the community. After the word got out that the station held a growing connection with and understanding of the community, Sonoma County's Chief Administrative Officer Rob Dice turned to KRCB to hold conversations about the thorny issue of jail overpopulation and how best to deal with it. This was the first time the county had sought out the station as a partner, and the connection had nothing to do with the station's programming or on-air capacity. Instead, the relationship came about because the station was viewed to have something valuable the community needs—a different way to approach and work in the community. Other partnerships with the Volunteer Center of Sonoma County and with the Community Foundation of Sonoma County soon followed, and as Dobbs says, "When they start thinking about community-engagement projects, they always pick up the phone and call us—it's the first thing they do."

KRCB was also contacted by the local Department of Public Health about partnering with the department and the nationally televised program called *Unnatural Causes*. Before occupying its new space, KRCB has told us, it would not have been asked. The station just wasn't on people's radar screen.

Once the discussion with the Department of Public Health began, KRCB used what it had learned from CEI to help shape the focus and approach of the partnership by suggesting additional partners—specifically, organizations dealing with health issues in low-income communities, including Community Action Partnership (CAP) and County Health Centers. As the partnership grew and developed, KRCB and CAP were invited to a national poverty conference in New Orleans to discuss their efforts. At the conference, Dobbs encouraged the poverty groups to seek out public broadcasters as partners in their work. Here, then, the station was viewed as being essential to the community in addressing a major *community* concern.

Much the same happened at WSKG, in Binghamton. When Brian Sickora took over as general manager, he found that the station's standing was so low among other community groups that he felt he had to "plead his case" just to be invited to some meetings. Organizations simply couldn't see why they would partner with WSKG. But, under Sickora's leadership, the station's growing understanding of the community and demonstrated commitment to creating impact has started to change the dynamic. He says, "The community perceives us differently. They're calling us to get us actively involved in things."

Over the past two years, WSKG has become a sought-after partner. Among the organizations asking to partner with the station is one of the most powerful and influential players in the community: Binghamton University. Recently, as the university contemplated launching a new civic engagement center, it sought out WSKG's expertise. Erik Jensen, the station's Director of Community Engagement, describes the situation in this way:

Binghamton University approached us early on. One of their vice presidents is creating a Center for Civic Engagement at the University. As they were beginning to move that concept from some initial planning and internal work, they started involving community entities and organizations. I believe we were one of the first for them to call in and say, "We're thinking about instituting and moving forward with a Center for Civic Engagement." They wanted to know what we thought about it, and if we would be supportive of it. That seemed to be very important to them. That's one of those indicators—there's a major economic development engine, an entity that's so important to our region, and as they move forward with a major initiative, [they're] thinking about public broadcasting very early on as a potential partner and organization that they should be reaching out to. That was really strong evidence of us moving forward in the way we were hoping to regarding community engagement.

As this book went to press, the new center has become a reality and WSKG continues to be among the key partners working with the center's founding director, Allison Alden.

In a few short years, WSKG has gone from needing "to make the case" to being a sought-after partner recognized throughout the community as a key player. For Sickora and Jensen, these changes are a direct result of the station turning outward. Rather than simply looking for funding to support its programs, the station starts with the community's aspirations and concerns and demonstrates how it has a unique ability to understand and meet them.

Different groups have tapped WSKG's outward turn in different ways. The Aging Futures Project, a nationally recognized consortium on aging, asked WSKG to participate in a major national grant to integrate public service media into the project, strengthening the proposal and its reach throughout the region. In KSKG's partnership with the League of Women Voters and the local Chamber of Commerce to hold community candidate debates, the result, rather than run-of-the-mill podium exercises, included on-air Community Conversations both the night before *and* the night after each debate. More recently, WSKG, joining with several local organizations in the Working on Wellness (WOW) initiative to promote better health habits in the region, secured $150,000 in funding from the Conrad and Virginia Klee Foundation to move this partnership and the program from concept to reality.

For Illinois Public Media, the tables have turned as well. Of the changing local dynamic, General Manager Mark Leonard says:

> We're being invited to be at the table in dialogues where we've never been before. We've been invited to come to an ongoing conversation on the subject of sustainability. That endeavor is a combination of the Chamber of Commerce and the University of Illinois, Office of Engagement. Suddenly we were seen as a player. They are looking to us to participate given our expertise in engagement and our stature as a trusted community institution.

In St. Louis, KETC's different approach to working with local partners for *Facing the Mortgage Crisis* helped reinforce the fact that the station offered far more than its broadcast tower. Amy Shaw, Vice President of Education Services, has found that potential partners are starting to realize just how much more. "I think we're seen differently by potential partners in the community, something beyond a media organization or beyond television. So we kind of have a whole new bag of tricks to say, 'Listen, there's more to it than just a TV show.'" She added:

> *I think our relationship with a lot of our partners has changed. There's more back and forth and give and take, a lot more of thinking about the competencies of each organization, and partners thinking about us not just as media. The Federal Reserve Bank I think is the best example of that. You know, we didn't have an existing relationship with the Federal Reserve Bank prior to* Facing the Mortgage Crisis. *But through that relationship, they really saw a lot of the things that we were able to do in the community, and they were hoping to do the same things. It made them realize that we're aligned in so many ways, and made them realize "Wow, this is an organization that is well beyond television, there's so much more to them than just media. So how could we work together to think of the community at large?"*

A Trusted Convenor

A common thread running through many of these stories is the role that stations began to play as trusted community convenor. For many stations, the recognition of their potential as a convenor unlocked an untapped asset. In communities where connections between organizations or leaders are often rare, frayed, or nonexistent, these stations were able to convene groups across boundaries and create needed spaces for conversation. The stations found that creating such a space within the community was a role few occupied, and one that was desperately needed. As we noted earlier, public broadcasting stations are usually viewed by others as "safe" organizations—groups that are not in direct competition for attention, funding, and other forms of support. Who better to convene a meeting of groups from across the community? Here are just a few additional examples, beyond those that we have already highlighted.

KBPS is a classical music radio station serving the Portland, Oregon, area. The station came to CEI focused on strengthening the health of the classical music community in Portland. As it turned outward, it came to see the goal as one of strengthening the health of the community *through* classical music. Here's how the station put its new understanding:

> *To provide the tools and direction needed to assist the local classical world in forging better communication and cooperation; to provide the table (whether literal or virtual) around which they will meet and to ensure that those meetings are as productive as possible, so that they can create varied partnerships and programs to increase community participation. In many cases, individual organizations have already thought through their own responses to the issue. What they appear to need is a way to benefit from knowledge of other organization's responses, and opportunities to work as partners with each other. Some are already doing this. But the opportunities for creating ever-widening circles of partnership are abundant and largely untapped.*

As KBPS convened the first meetings, it discovered a wealth of innovation, talent, and commitment among other arts organizations and leaders in the community. But the station did not seek to create a new program or initiative; instead, in this instance, it was the convenor and connector. KBPS helped the community discover something essential about itself and helped it create the conditions to act together. Interestingly, many of the meetings actually took place in a bar, rather than in the station's conference room, or some other "official" place.

Another example of the power and potential of public broadcasters as convenors comes from Maryland Public Television. During a documentary about gay teens, the station asked participants who were leaders of local organizations that worked with gay teens to answer phone calls immediately following the show. This enabled viewers to connect to needed resources right away—often talking to the very person they had just seen in the documentary. But perhaps even more important, few of the organizations that the station brought together to discuss the situation of gay teens had ever been in the same room. Now, through the station's efforts, a network began to form. In this way, the station found that it could use its assets to build community. By convening these groups, the station gave them a space to connect and share ideas and insights. As one MPT producer said, "We should do this with all our shows."

The station in fact has adopted the same approach to a show on youth foster care in Maryland. Before starting work on the show, MPT asked key organizations within the state how it could best help engage communities on foster-care issues, beyond simply airing a program. The organizations said they needed help putting on Community Conversations to discuss the subject *before* the show aired. Now, working with these community partners, MPT is helping to convene local events around the state, using clips from the upcoming documentary as a way to frame public discussion.

Based in Los Angeles, KUSC had to overcome several sizable

barriers before it could become a sought-after partner for arts organizations in the Coachella Valley, California. Just prior to joining CEI, KUSC had established a "repeater station" in the valley that would carry the broadcast signal from its Los Angeles station. But trying to deepen its relevance to the valley's local arts community proved a real challenge. To begin with, the Los Angeles station is situated more than a two-hour drive from the Coachella Valley. In addition, the local arts community in the valley is highly fragmented. What's more, many of the key players in the arts community wanted to have little to do with one another. Still others chafed at the idea that a single valley community existed at all. Each town and city saw its interests as entirely separate from others.

Given these challenges, KUSC set out to create a space where the disparate arts groups could safely meet and talk about the kind of arts community each wanted for the valley. KUSC started by asking about people's aspirations to help create common ground and prevent the conversation from devolving into a replay of earlier personal conflicts and turf wars. Through its work, and because of its status as a neutral convenor, KUSC helped build a network of arts groups that began to work together and think about community.

According to the station's Director of Development, Janet McIntyre, these meetings became so successful that "one of the major, major arts organizations that had never agreed to partner in any other organization's fundraising or other activities contacted *us* to participate in what we're doing. They think our work is worthwhile, and they want to be a part of it. It's a major victory for us."

In Illinois, even before CEI, the Illinois Public Media was seen as a national leader among public broadcasters in terms of its engagement efforts. But inside the station, these efforts often operated in a vacuum—separated from other core functions. Worse yet, many in the station saw "community engagement" as a high-cost, low-return proposition. Not the easiest of circumstances for an organization about to embark with us and fellow stations in CEI's multi-year effort.

When the station started with CEI, it wanted to expand its Youth Media Workshop, a program for at-risk youth that taught roughly a dozen students how to make radio and TV documentaries. But after a few months into CEI, a different set of questions began to bubble up within the station. Whereas past conversations about the Youth Media Workshop focused on how to build on the success of the *program*, now the question was, what impact do we want to have in the community? in working with youth.

As Kimberlie Kranich, Director of Community Engagement, and Mark Leonard, General Manager, and others at the station wrestled with this question, it was clear that while the Youth Media Workshop was a popular and positive program for the dozen or so students involved, it fell well short of the community impact that people at the station had begun to want. The station now aspired to use its assets and capacity to create opportunities and change in the lives of vulnerable youth communitywide.

By turning outward, and asking fundamentally different questions, the station came to realize just how frayed the networks between and among the various organizations and individuals working with youth were. While there were many groups and efforts underway, there was a lack of common purpose and few ties between and among one another. The station determined that simply producing more programming would have little impact on building these ties, or, indeed, on improving the lives of children throughout the community. But as a neutral convenor, the station could bring together the concerned groups and the community.

For many leaders of the groups, it was the first time they'd ever met one another, despite living in the same community and working on similar issues. Convening these leaders over time has helped create new connections and possibilities that the previous approach to Youth Media Workshop never could have supported. In the meantime, the station is now leveraging the documentary projects from the students enrolled in the Youth Media Workshop; these pieces now inform the meetings and community efforts the station convened.

One of the most heartwarming examples of a station re-thinking its potential as a convenor comes from WTIP in Grand Marais, Minnesota. Many of WTIP's efforts as part of CEI focused on creating spaces for people in the community to engage in productive conversations around the community's most contentious issues. Earlier we highlighted the station's work in creating the *First Thursday* program around these goals. But the station still went further to use the same perspective to shape its own space. WTIP embedded its desire to enable the community to come together and form new connections into the very design for its new station building. Here's the way Deb Benedict, WTIP's General Manager, explains how the station turned its building into a much needed space for the community:

Based on what we learned from the Community Engagement Initiative, and what role we wanted to play in the community, we set this building up not as ... just an office building where people come to work, but as a community center.

In taking this approach, Benedict said that she and her colleagues wanted to know: "How we could design our role in the community as a convenor" in a way that could "be a role model for other organizations." She continued, now reflecting on how the new building is working out:

> With our interviews and our community calendar shows, we have people coming and going; they sit in our little lobby and converse with each other. This building has become a spot where people are coming and going all day, be it citizens, journalists, or different folks that represent organizations coming in for interviews. We regularly hold events here for folks to come to.... Based on what we had learned through the community-engagement process, we wanted to be more of a center for folks rather than just an isolated office facility.

Taking it still another step further, WTIP recently applied for and received a grant that helped the station create a community garden on station grounds:

> [We worked] with community partners to dig up a section of our parking lot and with the local lumberyard to get some chips and create soil, getting manure from local horse people. A local contractor dug up the parking lot, filled it in, brought rock in. Then we [worked] with a local gardening group in selecting people who would actually be doing the community garden.

And as you might expect, the garden has become another place where people in the community can meet, talk, and connect with one another. This includes kids from a nearby child-care center.

Deb says, "There's nothing better than seeing local kids from the daycare center who have a plot in our garden come up with their daycare providers and come and water their garden and pick their peas, and that sort of thing." Now, people are congregating at the station, making it a local hub of activity—both on air and off.

CHAPTER 9

THE SECRET TO INTERNAL CHANGE

It is a relentless outward *focus that best creates the conditions for and ultimately drives internal change—and not the other way around. Focusing inward will never produce a turn outward.*

Y OU CANNOT TURN OUTWARD by focusing inward. And yet, isn't this what so many groups and organizations set out to do? They undertake internal change efforts all in the name of engaging the community or improving their relevance and significance. Wasn't this the approach of most of the organizations we describe in Chapter III? But what is clear from CEI, and other Harwood efforts over the years, is that the very act of turning outward drives internal change; it is what prompts and guides organizations to find more effective ways of working internally, developing stronger norms, and crafting common language for pursuing their public mission. Internal change efforts that seek a deeper relationship with the community must be in service of something larger than simply revamping an organization yet one more time. It is a relentless *outward* focus that best creates the conditions for and ultimately drives internal change—and not the other way around.

This chapter details just a few of the numerous internal changes that resulted when CEI stations made the choices to turn outward. These changes placed the stations on a different trajectory—one that undoubtedly also brought about dissonance, ambiguity, and personal consternation for many station staff. Not only is this un-avoidable, we believe it *must* be welcomed. CEI stations found that creating change in the community meant being willing to accept change in the station.

New Spaces within Stations

We saw that as each station developed its community efforts, it quickly recognized the need to create new community spaces that could foster different kinds of conversations and enable different types of connections. The same was true of spaces within the stations themselves. Few stations had internal spaces that could span boundaries dividing departments and enable departments to share information and ideas in a way that promoted innovation. We found that stations that were able to pry open new spaces for fundamentally different kinds of conversations about their work and its impact made the greatest strides in terms of internal change.

As the need for new internal spaces became more and more apparent, we introduced something we call "Innovation Spaces." These "spaces" are defined more by their characteristics[3] than by physical space or a particular process. Innovation Spaces emerged from more than 20 years of Harwood experience in creating room for reflection, learning, and innovation. They were based on the need for a radical shift in internal relationships and conversations, a shift from endless critiques, even criticism, to an intentional focus on creating something together. Innovation Spaces asked participants to shift from reflexively asking, "what do we need to do?" a question that inevitably produces yet more activities and efforts to control things, to asking, "What are we learning" and "What does this mean for us?" This second set of questions creates a far different conversation, one that leads to deepening insights, making sense of ideas and conversations, and ultimately fostering and producing innovation.

Since Innovation Spaces were designed to give rise to certain kinds of conversations, stations adapted these spaces to fit their own contexts. In this way, the spaces became a part of each station and arose from its particular context and challenges, spurring

---

3 See the Appendices, page 169, for the characteristics of Harwood Innovation Spaces.

further innovation than if there had been a single prescriptive, one-size-fits-all approach.

As much as any of the CEI stations, KETC in St. Louis made determined use of Innovation Spaces. For Amy Shaw, Vice President of Education Services, and Dale Berenc, Manager of Education Services, these spaces quickly became an essential part of advancing their work with the community. In a station memo about CEI, they wrote:

> *The concept of the Innovation Spaces has been embraced as an important way to internalize the concepts of CEI. A group of eight station staff have been identified to come together in a protected space on a weekly basis to discuss what we're learning in our new way of working together and in the community. The team working on KETC's* Facing the Mortgage Crisis *decided to meet every morning, a radical departure from their normal approach. The focus of these meetings was also new: they asked whether their efforts were helping or hindering their connection with community. These meetings and the new questions created new norms for how work could get done at the station. Now other staff members sought out these morning meetings because it has become known as the space where mission-driven conversations take place. Cross-functional teams have become the norm.*

KETC found Innovation Spaces so valuable that it reclaimed an underused portion of the station's building to serve as a permanent home for these conversations. Here's how Shaw and Berenc wrote about the potential for this new space:

> *We know that innovation happens when people work and learn*

together to make things happen. To that end, we're taking an underutilized space in the station and turning a portion of that space into our Innovation Space. Once the space is created, this group will gather around the idea of innovating—to think about the work we do as a station team in a new way and how that work impacts the community... and to incorporate what we're learning about our community to develop common language around this learning.

Of course, the Innovation Spaces weren't always a hit immediately. At Illinois Public Media, the first few conversations fell short and frustrated some participants. Station staff wanted to see immediate and concrete action steps to take. General Manager Mark Leonard previously had stuck with Community Conversations. Now he stuck with the Innovation Space, seeking to push through the initial doubt and reticence. Again, his persistence was rewarded. After just a few conversations, he noticed that "more people are attending them than when we first started and the conversations are more meaningful and deep." Leonard found himself surprised by "how excited staff was to be part of Innovation Space conversations." One of these staff members went on to tell him, "I feel myself being able to be more honest in my conversations with colleagues. My comfort level is a little higher. If I need to be brutally honest, I can do that."

For Illinois Public Media and many other stations, creating these kinds of spaces where staff could be more honest and productive was critical for working across organizational lines and giving rise to a different way for staff to talk about the station and their work.

At Vermont Public Television, Station Programmer Kelly

Luoma and Community Outreach Director Elizabeth Ottinger created their own variation of a Harwood Innovation Space. As in other CEI stations, the meetings have become a regular part of how the station works, providing an important place for people to explore how the station can shift, as Luoma and Ottinger would put it, from "broadcasters to public media organizations with broadcasting assets." These conversations also enabled the station to work across departmental boundaries, which had slowed progress for years. Here's Luoma's description of how they now work at VPT:

> Since CEI, we have an internal committee … that's a multidiscipline, multidepartmental committee. We meet every month, after Public Square airs to talk about the next shows that are coming forward and how we're specifically going to integrate, not only online, but community engagement into both [on-air and online] components.

In the past, Maryland Public Television struggled to engage staff in conversations other than those focused exclusively on programming. So, when the station set up one of its first Innovation Spaces, the organizers had reason for trepidation. But to their surprise, things started to change once the Innovation Space got off the ground. Having a place for creative conversation where learning, and not simply delegating, was the goal, met a deep need among many in the station. It was finally an opportunity to create and innovate and remember why we're here.

MPT now has regular Innovation Space meetings, and the initial doubts have been erased as the meetings now can draw more than 70 people. These conversations are devoted to examining ways to engage with the community meaningfully; and instead of people leaving such meetings because they are "not about programming," station managers report that staff members stay engaged throughout.

Tearing Down Walls

As we mentioned earlier, before we launched CEI, many public broadcasters and interested observers warned us that public broadcasting stations were highly fragmented and worked in silos. Those warnings were accurate—and then some! However, rather than taking this challenge head-on by implementing a new *internal* change process at the risk of never having impact beyond the station and maybe producing no results, we helped stations turn outward and focus on community impact. As we had anticipated, this reorientation and renewed focus on community impact prompted new internal relationships and spurred cross-departmental collaboration because it allowed staff to fulfill its aspirations for the work. Again, internal change was a result of turning outward.

Take the situation at KRCB in Sonoma County. Before CEI, interactions between production staff and outreach staff were rare and sometimes tense. One leader at the station said that at the outset of CEI, production staff could barely "tolerate" outreach efforts. Norms for collaboration were missing, as were conversations about the station as a whole. True collaboration seemed unlikely at best.

By design, CEI was hard to pigeonhole as belonging solely to outreach or education or any other single department or program. Because CEI was more than a project, it cut across stations in ways that other previous efforts had not. This in itself worked to breakdown the strict separation between programming and outreach and other departments. But for KRCB the real turning point was when staff came together to talk about their aspirations for the community. Talking about aspirations created an opening for departments to forge a sense of common purpose—one rooted *outside* the building. KRCB's General Manager, Nancy Dobbs, found that these conversations produce "a stronger sense of station mission" and "allow us to connect a little more in the hallway" and "make a difference inside the station."

Now KRCB producers ask at the outset of production meetings, "How can we connect this with the community?" In fact, the local programming producer now regularly blogs and seeks community comments—another small but important sign of people turning outward.

Without reconfiguring internal relationships, stations could not have met their new community goals, seized new opportunities, or deepened their local significance. To see this, let's look again at Nashville's documentary series *Next Door Neighbors*. At the Nashville station, turning outward and holding Community Conversations before producing the first documentary was a radical departure from business as usual. For years documentaries followed a fairly conventional process: producers would pick the topic, map out content, identify and interview experts, shoot the story, and then hand it over to the outreach staff to push the product out into the community.

Next Door Neighbors turned this process upside-down. Producers and programmers together started out in the community, holding Community Conversations to understand how people in the community think about and define relevant issues to them. These conversations led to a new framing and new sources, which yielded better content. Production staff and other people within the station have taken notice, as NPT Vice President Kevin Crane explains:

> *When you do something and it works, we don't have anybody saying, "You know we shouldn't be doing that anymore." It's very nice to be reaping the rewards now and the recognition now even within the building: "Boy that was some project, and that really got people's attention." That's really nice, and the Community Engagement Initiative was a big part of that.*

Crane says that the success of the *Next Door Neighbors* has been the catalyst for altering the way people inside NPT do their work:

> *Outreach was something the outreach department used to do. Now the production people don't see it that way. They question more the need to just speak to a community leader, to find the expert. They don't just automatically assume, "Well, I've got to find the person who will tell me what the community thinks." They're much more comfortable now with the idea, "I'll just go talk to people." We keep hearing from people at restaurants, and local businesses, "Oh yeah, he's [a documentary producer who was previously highly skeptical of CEI] great. He comes in and he hangs out and has coffee." He's not sitting there with a camera or a tape recorder; he's just out there talking to people.*

Perhaps most tellingly, one of Crane's fellow producers told him, "[I] can't imagine doing a documentary without first doing Community Conversations."

Across the board, stations are working differently because they turned outward. Like many of his peers at other stations, John King, General Manager of Vermont Public Television, sees progress, but knows there is even more to do:

We still have relapses, but I think we've come so far from where we were. Because now, with the various groups that we've set up, and the various committees, interdisciplinary teams are involved in a lot of these decisions that used to be made on a department by department basis.

Years of department infighting and resentment didn't just melt away. Initial reticence and tension gave way to new relationships and new work practices only by shifting the focus to creating external change. When staffs turned outward, they recognized that different departments held similar aspirations for the work, and that to have the community impact they wanted meant they needed to change how they worked internally.

Changes in Staffs and Boards

An outward orientation can also bring a need to restructure staffing roles and departments, or to reassign, even fire, staff in order to assemble a team capable of creating community impact. This is what happened at some stations as CEI unfolded. Simply put, to create change you must be willing to endure and embrace the implications and dissonance of change.

At Illinois Public Media, Mark Leonard undertook an examination of long-standing work arrangements to see whether they fit with the station's new focus on community. For instance, he redesigned how he staffs his public radio station, which meant the end of some long-time programming, such as a classical music program which was replaced with a satellite service. In this instance, seeing the opportunity to take advantage of a strong staff person, Leonard reassigned the former classical music host to be out in the community instead of inside the station, behind a microphone. In other cases, staff was moved to new departments. Yet other people who did not want to be part of the new approach found new employment. As he says:

> *People are beginning to believe that this is not just going to go away. They can't outwait it. They have to incorporate it in their thinking. It's part of us finding relevance going forward because we know we are facing really difficult economic times. And people are willing to accept a plan, an organizing principle—they're probably thirstier for it now.*

But there's more. As the station began to make great strides in its CEI work, Leonard realized that one of the best ways to spread the ideas and the approach internally was for the staff to capture and tell their own stories of change. So, he assigned one of his reporters to "cover" the story. The story was never intended for an outside audience; instead, it helped remind staff of the incredible changes they had made. By documenting the transformation, indeed by dedicating resources to tell the station's own story, Leonard sent a powerful signal about the importance and priority of the work.

In Binghamton, WSKG General Manager Brian Sickora determined that leading the station's efforts in the community required a different skillset within his staff. Rather than trying to tack these efforts onto an existing job, he made the decision to dedicate scarce resources to hiring a new person, Erik Jensen, to be Director of Community Engagement. Jensen came from the local United Way, where his years of experience meant he could bring a deep knowledge of the community to the station. Together, Sickora and Jensen revamped the old "outreach" department to have a new "engagement" thrust, refocusing the mission and work the department does. Dedicating time, energy, and financial resources to make engagement a key part of the station's capacity sends a clear signal to the rest of the station. As Jensen says, "Brian is walking the talk."

In Nevada, to help reinforce the outward turn of KNPR, Flo Rogers revamped the incentive structure at her station, embedding one of the key Harwood frameworks—The 3A's of Public Life[4]— into all performance evaluations. Changing job descriptions and evaluations helped engage and spur station staff to think more seriously about KNPR's effort to be *the* public media source in Nevada. Staff members are now expected to identify how they are contributing to improving a set of community-impact indicators as part of their annual review.

In addition to changing how she judges performance, Rogers found, as she puts it, that "The focus on impact in Las Vegas also

---

4 The 3A's of Public Life are touchstones for leaders who want to have impact and remain true to their core beliefs. The 3A's are: Authority, Authenticity, and Accountability. But to leaders who have used Harwood work, these words have different meanings that the common definitions. *Authority* is not about a person's title, power or education, rather it's about having a deep understanding of the community. In a world where people try to distort and manufacture reality, *authenticity* is about our willingness to see and hear reality and to reflect that in our work. Do people believe we're a part of the community, or a part from it. *Accountability* is not about placing blame or counting variables—it's fundamentally a question of whether our word is worth something. What promises have you made and are you living up to them?

allowed us to assign additional resources to expand our publication *Desert Companion* and designate a full-time Community Relations director-level position." What's more, "CEI has helped us create clear position descriptions for our Community Relations staff— something with which we had previously struggled."

CEI stations not only changed internal staffing, tasks, and performance reviews, but also how they worked with their Community Advisory Boards. Many found that by involving their boards in a different way, or by changing the composition of the boards, they could deepen the boards' impact. For KRCB in Sonoma, asking the Community Advisory Board to play a more dynamic role in the community energized the board and led to a flurry of action. Board members stepped up and began to call other organizations in town to learn about their work and deepen the station's connection to others in the community. By orienting the board's efforts outward—instead of continuing endless discussions about "programming" and internal matters—the Community Board finally found it had a substantial and essential role to play for the station.

At both KNPR in Nevada and KETC in St. Louis, station leaders realized that their Community Advisory Boards were not properly configured to support the station's new focus on community impact. The board composition needed to change if the stations were going to use their boards to help them establish a broader and deeper connection with the community. So, as with their other resources, the stations worked to find ways that their Community Advisory Boards could support the stations' outward turn and deepen their community impact.

Beyond the composition of the Community Advisory Boards, both KETC and KNPR changed how they saw and used these boards. As Amy Shaw of KETC, says, "Fundamentally, the boards became a listening tool—we listen to these people instead of simply telling them about our work. It is more meaningful now." By turning outward KETC recognized that its Community Advisory Board represented another asset, another way to understand and ultimately impact the community. At KNPR Rogers and others recognized that their Community Advisory Board enabled the station to reach further into the community. She says that instead of simply "fulfilling the requirements of reporting out to a representative group of community members," now the station is "talking with the Nevada Public Radio Community Advisory Board in terms of their board's extended networks in the community."

Support from the Top

To repeat: Internal change arises from an outward turn. But make no mistake—driving internal change requires support from top station leaders, including general managers, stations managers, and other senior staff. For instance, while KETC in St. Louis was effective at every step of the way, it made a significant leap forward following a February 2008 CEI meeting attended by General Manager Jack Galmiche. His presence and subsequent involvement accelerated the station's already impressive progress. Here's Amy Shaw, Vice President of Education Services, on the need for support from the top:

> *The bottom line is, without good leadership in the organization, this won't happen. Good people can want this to happen inside the organization—it just won't. It has to come from a leadership*

level. Generally, that's the CEO or other senior staff, but good leadership is imperative in this. I just don't think it works without it.

Clarity and conviction on the part of top station leaders are critical in demonstrating that this new way of thinking about the community—and this new way of thinking about the space that public broadcasters occupy in the community—is more than just a fad. Transformative changes like those at Illinois Public Media and KNPR in Nevada would not have been possible without strong support from their general managers. In both cases, the station general managers made clear the direction in which the station was moving and directly involved themselves in the day-to-day work of CEI.

Here's Mark Leonard of Illinois Public Media: "You have to have the top person in the organization—not just in lip service committed, but invested, participating consistently in all of the meetings, the strategies; they have to own it."

Years of new projects and siloed approaches to production have left many public broadcasters with myriad competing priorities. This is a common challenge for many civic-minded organizations: staff members spend their days stretched thin—with too much to do, too few resources, and too many problems to solve, and, critically, with too little sense of a clear public purpose. In Los Angeles, KUSC General Manager Brenda Barnes recognized that to create internal change she needed to step forward and clarify the station's priorities:

Whenever you're starting something new in any organization, it's an uphill battle. People tend to have a lot on their plates anyway.

There's a lot of stuff that people look at and say, "We should be doing this, or that, or the other thing." Everyone has their own opinion. So part of the role of a manager is to say, "Here's where we're going to spend our time and effort and here's why."

In thinking about internal change, our friends at Vermont Public Television remind us of something we have said throughout this book, but which could easily be lost when talking about "support from the top." Inside the organization, change emerges from people getting on the same page, working toward common efforts. And the need to get people's involvement from *across* a station is echoed in VPT's final CEI memo:

Leading change is often directed at the head of an organization. Although important, it takes more than one person to make change happen. It takes a leadership team committed to the vision to overcome the inertia of an organization steeped in a legacy model of broadcast. At VPT, we need to get all of our managers on board with this organizational change. Without that, we are creating paths of resistance.

So, one more time: To create strong internal change, turn outward.

CHAPTER 10

THE COMMUNITY-IMPACT TEST:
NEW QUESTIONS & METRICS

We're still in that position where a board member will say to me, "I don't understand why you're doing this. How does this make them listen to the radio?..." How does this build your audience?" And the answer is, it's not about building audience, it's about serving the community.

FLO ROGERS
GENERAL MANAGER
KNPR, LAS VEGAS

I N OUR WORK OVER THE YEARS we've come to know that systemic and sustainable change—that is, change that is deep and lasting and meaningful—comes about only when people see that there is a different set of choices and judgments that they need to make in doing their work. Only then does the focus and quality of their discussions change. Only then does their decision making and execution shift. It is only then that people truly turn outward. This was surely the case in CEI.

There were two distinct but related mechanisms that helped CEI stations realign their existing decision making and priority setting with their focus on community. The first was discovering a different set of questions that focused them squarely and intentionally on community and their alignment with it. The second involved their use of new metrics to gauge whether they were having impact and, if not, to recalibrate their efforts based on what they were learning to ensure they were making a genuine difference.

Both of these "community-impact" mechanisms required a willingness to make new choices and judgments. There was no way around it. What's clear is that when CEI stations took genuine ownership of these choices and judgments, their efforts gained traction, and the trajectory of their work and their relationship with the community fundamentally changed.

Asking Different Questions

Oftentimes productive change starts by simply asking the right question. A good example is KETC of St. Louis, which asked new questions that they created initially to stay focused and aligned with their turn outward. Today, these questions continue to drive their work. Now they routinely ask:

• *How can* KETC*'s community-engagement efforts become better linked to daily operations?*

• *How can our efforts lead to greater community significance, where* KETC *is more involved and engaged in the community?*

• *How can our efforts lead communities to view* KETC *as a trusted and essential leader?*

• *How will the public challenges in our region get addressed through our approach to our work?*

• *How can we strengthen our community?*

For KETC, these questions were central to creating "authentic community engagement efforts that measurably improve the civic health of our region." Notice the focus of these questions and their language. The questions are not about how the station can increase its viewership or audience; nor do they focus on how to make more effective on-air pledge drives. It's not that KETC somehow became selfless or disinterested in its organizational health; rather, what these questions illustrate is that KETC thinks of its connection to the community as the driving force for all its work. This is how Amy Shaw, KETC's Vice President of Education Services, framed her evaluation of the station's future:

If we apply the same strategies that we've applied over the last 30 or 40 or 50 years, we're not going to be successful in the long term.

*So I think the big bet for us is the success of our entire organization,
the success of our community... and to us engagement is really
going to be the answer to that.*

At KETC, staying focused on community impact while working on *Facing the Mortgage Crisis* was a *daily* challenge. Each day
presented new hurdles and obstacles and new demands for keeping people in the station onboard. Shaw and her colleague Dale
Berenc, Manager of Education Services, knew that to keep the
team focused meant regularly reminding it about the station's
new intentionality. As Shaw told us:

*It goes back to those very, very clearly articulated purposes of
our involvement in CEI. Everything we did started with restating
those purposes. They were posted on the wall at every meeting we
had. [Staff would] point on the wall and say, "Okay, here's what
we're driving towards. Tell me how what you're doing is driving
towards that purpose."*

Building upon the success of *Facing the Mortgage Crisis*, Shaw
now believes the station has changed "the kind of work we do, the
kinds of projects we take on. Now we are not looking at anything
without looking at the impact we have."

Across the CEI stations, the types of questions that KETC has
asked are regularly being asked, questions that get at the heart
of what it means to turn outward. The questions focus on how
stations can align their resources and capacities with their efforts
to create community impact. These questions are helping shape
the internal culture of stations, and they are enabling stations to
support and create *with* the community a new civic culture.

Before CEI, Maryland Public Television used an internal project review form to evaluate new efforts. It was very simple. Staff simply checked off a box stating, "The initiative meets organizational mission." Before CEI, this was fine, and for some it might even have allowed them to feel as though the station was "turning outward." But all that has changed. Now, after CEI, staff members are expected to *explain* how a project actually meets the station's strategic plan, and, more important, how the project connects to a *community* priority and concern. This new test has spurred different questions at the station, where the general manager, production staff, and others ask, "How can our association with this issue have the greatest impact in the community?" Once again, the question is not about the station itself but about community impact. Recall the leaders in Chapter III who said, "I'm not evaluated by how well I involve people. Keeping my job depends on what we get done." In these stations, community impact and involving people became part of "getting things done."

The same focus on generating community impact came to shape efforts at KRCB in Sonoma County. There, the station altered the criteria used to make choices and judgments about programming and other efforts. Just as happened at Maryland Public Television and KETC in St. Louis, a new set of questions is now reshaping what the station does. General Manager Nancy Dobbs says they now ask "whether 'this activity' or 'that activity' or 'that program' will further community understanding in some way or another." She goes on to say, "What we're trying to do is build our capacity, and hopefully the community's capacity, to connect with one another. That's the real challenge."

Still another example comes from Illinois Public Media. Here, the staff identified what they describe as the "four big questions" to ensure the station stays focused on serving as a catalytic or boundary-spanning organization in the community. These questions illustrate a new way of seeing their relationship with the community. The questions they now ask are:

• *Is there programming we need to rethink (in what way)?*

• *In what ways can we build stronger connections between off-air and on-air?*

• *In what ways can we build stronger connections in the communities we serve?*

• *What work practices do we need to adopt to be catalytic?*

Ultimately, every new program produced at Illinois Public Media must pass what the station explicitly named its "community-impact test." And the station has put its money where its mouth is. Passing the community-impact test is a requirement for any program to receive funding. Thus, instead of making community impact an afterthought, something people might think about once an effort is already underway (which is too late for any meaningful change), Illinois Public Media ensures that the community stays front and center at all times from the very start. As the station's last memo to CEI makes clear, this means making hard choices about what the station does and why:

What are we going to give up? What are our priorities? We've made engagement a priority in FM but not across the institution. We have a culture here of not giving things up—we're not the best at prioritizing what to cut in relationship to what we should add—and we wear doing so much as a badge of honor.

Staying focused for KNPR in Las Vegas meant that Flo Rogers and her team had to check their tendency to expand efforts and scale—once station short-hand for *impact*. The success of their work with CEI and related efforts created a flood of new opportunities, but keeping to their focus on community impact has helped them evaluate these options in a larger context—that of the community. For instance, because of its work with CEI, the station chose not to expand into new areas they once thought promising. Here's Rogers:

The CEI project helped us steer the board away from acquiring a new license and expanding the broadcast footprint, toward deepening our relevance to our primary community in Las Vegas.... For the first 25 years of this organization, we grew by growing audiences [who were] listening to [our] transmitters. And our measure of how big the organization got was about how much radio content we deliver through our system of transmitters. When we got into the process of writing a three-year plan, it was very clear to us that the way this organization would move forward would be much more about deepening our relationship with our primary area of service, i.e., Las Vegas, and deepening that relationship as opposed to building audiences in other places to incrementally add to the footprint.... The challenge for me as the CEO is to connect the dots for my board of directors. We're still in that position where a board member will say to me, "I don't understand why you're doing this. How does this make them listen to the radio?... How does this build your audience?"And the answer is, it's not about building audience, it's about serving the community. *[Emphasis added.]*

For KNPR, the question is no longer, how does this make them listen to the radio? Now the question is, how is this serving the community? New questions are leading to new answers and new impact.

For Vermont Public Television, staying focused on impact is what enabled the station to be clear about purpose and to distinguish between "activity and action." Here's how VPT characterized the distinction in its final report as part of CEI:

We have the potential to change. We have the resources available to make that change, and we are on a path toward our vision. We need to push ourselves to create partnerships and content that not only inform but help people understand an issue, that start engaging conversations, that move people to take action or change behaviors. There has to be a purpose to our work; the purpose should be about the impact, not the activity.

To turn these goals into reality required VPT to return time and again to a focus on community and impact so that the station could make more intentional and, ultimately, more strategic choices. As Station Programmer Kelly Luoma observed:

One of the things we worked very hard on … is getting away from the outputs to really try and find the impact. To find the impact means you really have to have some sense of what you're hoping to accomplish by creating content or creating engagement. Oftentimes, we just did it [went ahead with a program]—and to have those conversations ahead of time, we continue to struggle with that, but it is something that we are really working on and committed to working on. And I think the other thing is—it's even before a project gets under way, it's thinking differently. It's not just doing something to do it, it's really trying to think through much more in depth than we ever have before ... and making sure that what we take on is truly strategic, and we understand why we're getting involved. This has really made us think differently, think far more strategically, think far more about the impact of taking on projects, work, and partnerships.

While station leaders like Luoma would like to see the station move faster to fully adopt this new way of thinking in their work, she say she recognizes the progress that the station has made. "We still struggle with coming up with what are the outcomes of a project, and whereas that didn't even exist in our minds or in our process before, it does now."

Like Leonard, Rogers, and Luoma, Joe Krushinsky, Vice President for Institutional Advancement at Maryland Public Television, also held a deep desire to create community impact, which forced him to face up to questions about his station's capacity and priorities, and which meant taking a different path than business-as-usual:

I think we have to be honest with ourselves. We can't be all things to all people. There are limitations to our capacity. So, we have to do a lot of good listening to stakeholders and with different groups in the community to understand what is important. And then do a realistic process of which of those issues we can address competently given our resources. And that necessarily means that some things that we've been doing as a matter of habit for 10, 20, 30 years might have to get a second look and drop off of our "do" list.

Before CEI, meetings at WPBT in Miami often devolved into turf battles—fights over programming time—that focused more on making programs than on making an impact. But that also is now changing, as Neal Hecker, Vice President for Programming, explains:

> *Negotiating internally with departments—we used to come in and everybody would fight for their piece of it [programming time], and now we're able to sit everybody down and say, "Okay, now let's step back from this. What is it that we're trying to accomplish here? Ultimately, what is it we want to do here?" And not, ultimately, what is the project we need to get done?*

Different questions are creating different kinds of conversations that are producing different results. Such questions serve to fundamentally shift the focus from producing *programming* to producing *impact*. They enable stations to turn outward. In every organization and community with which Harwood has worked over the years, it is the emergence of new kinds of questions like the ones we're now seeing within CEI stations that have been the hallmark of deep and lasting change. Organizations that change their questions are the ones that see change in their community.

New Metrics

The second major mechanism for helping stations stay turned outward was the use of metrics to determine whether a station's efforts were improving the civic health of their communities and deepening the station's local significance. To create metrics that fit required innovation and iteration. It was only by working directly with the CEI stations that we were able to craft metrics that reflected the essence and spirit of this work.

You should know that throughout the 1990s, the Harwood Institute strenuously argued against metrics for evaluating the kind of work done in CEI and other Harwood-related efforts. We felt that metric systems by and large failed to reflect or accurately measure how change occurs in communities. Too many metric systems simply ignored what we know constitutes evidence of emerging change. And too often, the blunt application of such systems led to the distortion of on-the-ground efforts, as practitioners attempted to contort themselves to satisfy funders and evaluators and, in the process, ultimately lost focus on making a difference. This still happens.

And yet, we fundamentally believe that each of us must personally account for the work we do and the pledges we make in public life and that it is incumbent upon us to know whether our work is creating the impact we seek, or promised. What's more, the CEI stations kept telling us they needed ways to gauge their progress and needed something they could point to that would enable them to share stories of impact with skeptical colleagues and community partners. So the question became: How could we devise metrics that genuinely reflect the essence and spirit of this work? How can we know whether our approaches were having a positive impact in the lives of people in communities? And if such efforts were having limited impact, how could the stations increase the likelihood of increased impact? Otherwise, what's the purpose of doing this work, right?

With this in mind, we worked and innovated with the stations to develop the Community-Impact Indicators, a method by which they could find, catalogue, and make sense of "proof points" to demonstrate their station's impact in the community. This tool used impact indicators that were relevant and significant to the stations on the one hand and tied to Harwood's definition of "civic health" on the other. In addition to developing the Community-Impact Indicators, we shared with the stations a previously created instrument, the Harwood Significance Barometer, a tool for helping stations or other organizations gauge their progress toward becoming a Boundary-Spanning Organization.[5]

The seven indicators listed below make up the Community-Impact Indicators. For each indicator, we set out possible benchmarks that a station can use to determine its progress over time. For the purposes of this discussion, we've listed only the seven indicators and not the accompanying benchmarks:

1. *Other groups in the community make commitments to act on the same public issue as our organization.*

2. *A growing network of organizations and leaders connects to us and to each other.*

3. *Clear connections exist between on- and off-air work, between Community Conversations and programming.*

4. *Expanded role for our organization in community.*

---

5 To see the traits of Boundary-Spanning Organizations go to page 171 in the Appendices.

5. *Recognition among key funders that their individual organizations need to invest their resources to impact civic health.*

6. *New work habits and practices appear in our organization; individuals are able to explain how engagement is relevant to their work.*

7. *Our organization has methods to capture, process, and learn from its experience.*

An especially strong emphasis was placed on how the stations could take what they were learning from their metrics and directly apply those insights into their daily efforts. In this way, the metrics were focused on "gaining new knowledge" and "learning," not just "counting" or even "measuring change."

While all of the stations used the Community-Impact Indicators, each applied the system differently. Typically, a station would choose two or three main indicators, along with relevant benchmarks that demonstrated change on the indicators. The unique context, challenges, and capacity of each station meant that it needed to make choices and judgments about which indicators and benchmarks would best help it create and measure the impact it sought.

In addition to providing indicators that any station could use to measure its progress, we also demanded that each station create a use of the metrics for its own purposes, instead of just adopting a blunt, one-size-fits-all cookie-cutter approach.

For example, after using the Community-Impact Indicators, Neal Hecker of WPBT in Miami, called the results an "ah-ha" moment. He came to see that the tool was "a place to start measuring, as a station, what others are doing. Very useful to hear other people concretely think about the benchmarks they are hitting, what they are doing to be helpful to other departments." For Hecker, the indicators were yet another way to break down walls within the station and create a sense of common purpose.

To fit its individual needs, Illinois Public Media found another use of the indicators. The station used them to gauge the progress of the network it convened of community groups that serve vulnerable youth. The consensus among the group was that it had not generated as much progress in the community as it would have hoped, which then spurred the group to rededicate and refine their collaboration. They currently are creating a first-ever "asset map" of groups serving at-risk youth in the community, so they can begin to identify strengths, gaps, and duplication in efforts. This use of the indicators is an example of how the stations have taken CEI tools beyond their walls, helping provide resources to others in the community to cultivate a different kind of public life.

The philosophical approach underlying the design of the metrics was that change occurs only over time and that the hope is to be able to see signs of progress along the way. This is what KRCB in Sonoma County, highlighted about the indicators in its final CEI memo:

> *Knowing and reassuring staff and the board that we are making change; that we are making a difference in the health of our community—certainly we will use the metrics we've developed, and will develop more specific ones to each project. We will need to*

remember that you can't always "see" progress of the sort we seek and that it will take a very long time.

Of course, "numbers" alone won't always be adequate reflections of progress; indeed, often they are not. So, the Community-Impact Indicators require stations to gather stories, conversations, and reflections as well as data. Joe Krushinsky, at Maryland Public Television has underscored this point:

Everyone is talking about impact. But the numbers don't always tell the stories, the stories tell the stories. From the beginning of new work, we say right away that we need quotes and other input both during and after the workshop and other efforts. We must be aware of information gathering from the first step.

CHAPTER 11

SUSTAINING
&
SPREADING

I'm very proud that, though we are going through pretty unprecedented financial stresses right now, including layoffs and salary reductions and all kinds of crazy stuff that's going on, none of that has interrupted this conversation, this focus on turning outward.

JOE KRUSHINSKY
VICE PRESIDENT FOR INSTITUTIONAL ADVANCEMENT
MPT, MARYLAND

BEFORE STARTING TO WRITE this book, and about nine months after the completion of the CEI project, we decided to interview staff members from each of the CEI stations to follow up with them and see whether they'd been able to stay turned outward. We braced ourselves for stories of stations and staff turning back inward, particularly given the worsening economic conditions. Past experience suggested to us that at least a few stations would have slowly backed off the ideas of CEI and returned to business-as-usual. We found that's not the case.

The people we interviewed spoke of their own turn outward as being permanent and essential to the health and survivability of public broadcasting. This doesn't mean stations haven't faced internal resistance, or that the faltering economy hasn't raised the stakes. But to a person, the CEI participants said there's no going back to the way things were.

These leaders told us that their reorientation toward community and the practices that go with it are now integrated into their view of their work. Neal Hecker at WBPT in Miami spoke for many of the station leaders when he told us, "I feel like I can't go back. I don't know the way back from here." And what about Joe Krushinsky who, you might remember, said:

> If you had asked me at the start what might be some of the things that could make this project go badly, or end prematurely that [unprecedented financial stress] would have been pretty close to the top of the list. "If we run into hard times people will run screaming from this. And focus on short-term survival."

Well, how is Maryland Public Television faring these days?

According to Krushinsky:

I'm very proud that, though we are going through pretty unprecedented financial stresses right now, including layoffs and salary reductions and all kinds of crazy stuff that's going on, none of that has interrupted this conversation, this focus on turning outward.

Then there's Kelly Luoma of Vermont Public Television, who recently sent us an e-mail to announce that the station had just received two awards for their engagement work, the first from the Association of Public Television Stations and the second from the National Alliance on Mental Illness. As she wrote, "This outside recognition has been inspiring to staff, to see the impact and opportunities for VPT as a public media organization working together with our community partners to address issues and challenges facing Vermonters."

The results of the 12 CEI stations are a signal to other public broadcasters and civic-minded organizations everywhere about the promise of turning outward.

What follows is a set of 11 recommendations for sustaining and spreading this type of work. While it may be tempting to pick and choose from the recommendations, in reality they are part of a single, interdependent approach to pursuing transformation, which applies to public broadcasting and, we believe, all organizations that want to connect with community.

You will notice that much of what we say here we have said before. What we offer here is a checklist. The recommendations come from our work with public broadcasting stations but are **critical steps for any group or organization interested in becoming more relevant to and having an impact in the community.**

1. Make the mantra "Turn Outward."

We have found that the simple phrase *turn outward* reorients public broadcasters and helps them move down a path for change. In fact, we have found this to be true with all sorts of civic-minded organizations. This phrase makes an entreaty to individuals and organizations to turn away from their pervasive inwardness and turn toward the community.

2. Start with aspirations.

The focus on aspirations—on the kind of community that public broadcasters want to help create—rooted CEI in something very real for people. Aspirations are not about "visioning" or "dreaming" but about those things we hold to be most valuable within us and among us. Focusing on aspirations helped public broadcasters articulate the very reasons they started working in public broadcasting in the first place. While turning outward helps people turn toward the community, aspirations provide the fuel and guidance for moving ahead.

3. Focus on community impact.

Once stations have turned outward, and they are clear on shared aspirations, they need to focus on creating community impact. Staying focused on community impact opened up a new way of thinking and acting for stations. They moved from seeing themselves solely as producers of programming to generators of new possibilities for leveraging their assets, in different combinations, and with different partners, to improve the civic health of their communities. This relentless drive toward community impact helped change the conversation about station priorities and pushed station staff to rethink long-held assumptions. Rather than hoping that myriad activities added up to impact, station staff began to start with community impact as a way to ensure that their different efforts made sense and would make a difference. Without the focus on community impact, stations risk sliding back into internally focused business-as-usual.

4. Innovating is essential.

To seize the opportunities that emerge from turning outward requires stations to innovate and create. Fundamentally, CEI at its essence was an effort in "creating." CEI's focus on innovation meant that stations were forced to consider their goals and adjust their efforts all along the way—over and over and over again. A focus on innovation—rather than on planning or process—meant that stations were required to make on-going choices, judgments, and recalibrations. Stations took ownership of their efforts and worked to ensure that they were on the right trajectory so they could create to have the impact they sought.

5. Get out into the community fast.

One of the most critical steps for public broadcasters was the one that took them through the station doors and out into the community. We know that when staff participated in Community Conversations, they learned about turning outward and moved toward community impact. For many public broadcasters, engaging with the community may seem daunting. But stations and others that delay engaging with the community will be delayed in producing results. Without taking this step—going out into the community—change is not possible.

6. For internal change, turn outward.

The relentless outward focus of CEI drove internal change, not the other way around. To spread this work it is essential to avoid sliding into typical internal change discussions. The key is to remain outwardly focused. Then build internal change around that newfound, outward focus.

7. Stay focused on impact with sensible metrics.

Demonstrating progress in engaging communities requires sensible metrics so people know whether their work is creating the impact they seek, or promised. The metrics CEI used enabled stations to gauge progress and share stories of impact with skeptical colleagues and community partners. They also helped stations remain focused on what's vital, rather than what's "nice" or "sounds good." Last, metrics enabled the stations to learn from their work and adjust their efforts to increase their impact.

8. Don't try to kill dissonance.

Change is never easy. Though we might wish otherwise, creating change in the community means being willing to accept change within stations (and other kinds of public organizations). Placing a station (or any organization) on a different trajectory always brings about dissonance, ambiguity, and personal consternation for a staff. Not only is this unavoidable, it must be welcomed. Stations cannot skirt tension and dissonance if they truly want to create change. And funders that support change must not fear this dissonance either.

9. Build teams from across the station.

One of the central benefits of CEI was that it helped break down walls within stations, as staff focused together on creating community impact. Most of the successful CEI efforts can be traced back to instances where staff from different departments and functions were brought together. Without reconfiguring internal relationships, stations will struggle to meet existing challenges, seize new media opportunities, and deepen their local significance.

10. Stay focused on mind-sets and practices.

At the heart of the changes created by the CEI stations is a development of new mind-sets and practices. After turning outward, stations found numerous roles for themselves in the community, which required new skills, reflexes, and capacities. Special attention needs to be given to the development of new mind-sets and practices—none of this happens by itself.

11. Ask, "What space are we trying to occupy?"

At the start of CEI, many stations viewed the content and programs they produce and air as their primary asset. A single pivotal question helped stations rethink their assets, capacity, and role: what space do you occupy in the community? This question asked stations to think about where they sit in relationship to others—their fit with others—rather than simply to impose themselves on the community. Instead of envisioning the community in relation to the stations, now the stations described their work in distinctly more public terms. Now, the stations were in relationship with their communities.

CHAPTER 12

THE OPPORTUNITY

Turning outward is about doing work in a fundamentally public way. It is a "practice" about how people choose to see and engage with communities and public life. Like any practice, it takes time to cultivate and develop.

THIS BOOK IS ABOUT being intentional in making judgments and choices, with the first and most critical choice being whether to turn outward. Without turning outward, it is not possible for any of us to see and hear and engage with our community, or fulfill our aspirations to make a difference. None of the changes these public broadcasting stations created could happen without turning outward.

We can say with confidence that individuals and organizations that choose to turn outward are more likely to be rooted in their communities, more likely to be relevant and significant in what they do, and more likely to take action that leads to real impact.

But choosing to turn outward is not a one-time choice. It's not something to be minimized. For, after reorienting ourselves, we must make our way down a new path, one that sets us on a fundamentally different trajectory of taking action. There will be choices to make all along this new path. So, we must face up to the unpredictable nature of creating change. And we must make choices and judgments as we go, for there is no single recipe for moving ahead.

Still, it is easy to slip back into inwardness. The pressure to focus inward is laced with promises that if we only undertake yet another strategic plan, rebrand our efforts once more, or focus once again on internal governance, that we'll satisfy our challenges of relevance and significance—all without having to fundamentally change the way we see the community. Now, none of these internal activities are unimportant; each, in its own way, is essential at the right time. But let's be clear: too often, they take on too much prominence and crowd out one's ability to turn outward.

So, if we want to impact our community, each and every day we will be presented with these pressures and these choices.

We have found that Harwood's Four Building Blocks for Turning Outward, which we set out in Chapter 1—know your community, focus on impact, span boundaries, cultivate public innovators—provide the basis for handling both pressures and choices. We review them here for you to consider.

Most fundamental among the judgments and choices we will face is to determine whether we will come to "know our community," to understand the context of our community: What questions will we ask, who will we engage, what will we do with what we learn in our everyday work and decisions? Furthermore, we must figure out how we can reconnect and reengage people with one another: Will we see people as mere inputs, even pawns, in our own organizational processes, or as independent actors who hold the power and potential to shape their own communities?

We must also be clear about the impact we wish to generate in our communities: Will we focus primarily (even unknowingly) on narrow organizational or programmatic goals, or on the aspirations and concerns of the community itself; and what choices will we make in helping create the conditions for change in our communities, especially when such work can be slow and difficult?

Then there is the challenge of "spanning boundaries": Will we reach across dividing lines and create spaces where we can see and hear all people? Will we have the courage to hold up a mirror to the community?

Finally, will we "cultivate public innovators"? Will we root our work in an urge to do good, and support those who do this work? Will we make room for a different kind of approach to public life and this work, or will we push it to the side?

Why We're Here is the story of how a collection of passionate, talented, and yes,—brave—individuals in public broadcasting turned outward, made such choices, and the extraordinary impact they created. It is a story of people and groups overcoming significant odds and obstacles. But it is not unique. This path can be taken by anyone, in any organization, in any community.

At the Harwood Institute, we know this because we have done it. We have helped to cultivate numerous boundary-spanning organizations over the years, from local United Ways to arts organizations; from public libraries to human services groups; from newspapers to local public education funds.

To find such Boundary-Spanning Organizations, one cannot turn to any single mailing list or national association. Instead, it is their approach to public life that makes them special. They are led by individuals who hold a burning desire to be rooted in their communities and for their efforts to make a difference in the lives of people. Intuitively, they sense that they must make a set of internal choices so they can effectively turn outward. They also know that trying to overly control efforts in communities will sacrifice getting into the flow of the community and seizing new opportunities.

Turning outward is about doing work in a fundamentally public way. It is a "practice" about how people choose to see and engage with communities and public life. Like any practice, it takes time to cultivate and develop. But it is something that anyone can learn, and that all of us can be good at. It's a choice we must make.

APPENDICES

A.

Introduction to the Public Broadcasting Act of 1967

Public Broadcasting Act of 1967, as amended
Subpart D—Corporation for Public Broadcasting
Sec. 396. [47 U.S.C. 396] Corporation for Public Broadcasting

(a) Congressional declaration of policy
The Congress hereby finds and declares that—

1. *it is in the public interest to encourage the growth and development of public radio and television broadcasting, including the use of such media for instructional, educational, and cultural purposes;*

2. *it is in the public interest to encourage the growth and development of nonbroadcast telecommunications technologies for the delivery of public telecommunications services;*

3. *expansion and development of public telecommunications and of diversity of its programming depend on freedom, imagination, and initiative on both local and national levels;*

4. *the encouragement and support of public telecommunications, while matters of importance for private and local development, are also of appropriate and important concern to the Federal Government;*

5. *it furthers the general welfare to encourage public telecommunications services which will be responsive to the interests of people both in particular localities and throughout the United States, which will constitute an expression of diversity and excellence, and which will constitute a source of alternative telecommunications services for all the citizens of the Nation;*

6. *it is in the public interest to encourage the development of programming that involves creative risks and that addresses the needs of unserved and underserved audiences, particularly children and minorities;*

7. *it is necessary and appropriate for the Federal Government to complement, assist, and support a national policy that will most effectively make public telecommunications services available to all citizens of the United States;*

8. *public television and radio stations and public telecommunications services constitute valuable local community resources for utilizing electronic media to address national concerns and solve local problems through community programs and outreach programs;*

9. *it is in the public interest for the Federal Government to ensure that all citizens of the United States have access to public telecommunications services through all appropriate available telecommunications distribution technologies; and*

10. *a private corporation should be created to facilitate the development of public telecommunications and to afford maximum protection from extraneous interference and control.*

B.

Excerpted Remarks by
President Lyndon B. Johnson upon Signing
the Public Broadcasting Act of 1967

November 7, 1967

IT WAS IN 1844 THAT CONGRESS authorized $30,000 for the first telegraph line between Washington and Baltimore. Soon afterward, Samuel Morse sent a stream of dots and dashes over that line to a friend who was waiting. His message was brief and prophetic and it read: "What hath God wrought?"

Every one of us should feel the same awe and wonderment here today. For today, miracles in communication are our daily routine.... Today our problem is not making miracles—but managing miracles. We might well ponder a different question: What hath man wrought—and how will man use his inventions?

The law that I will sign shortly offers one answer to that question.

It announces to the world that our Nation wants more than just material wealth; our Nation wants more than a "chicken in every pot." We in America have an appetite for excellence, too. While we work every day to produce new goods and to create new wealth, we want most of all to enrich man's spirit. That is the purpose of this act.

It will give a wider and, I think, stronger voice to educational radio and television by providing new funds for broadcast facilities.

It will launch a major study of television's use in the Nation's classrooms and their potential use throughout the world. Finally—and most important—it builds a new institution: the Corporation for Public Broadcasting.

The Corporation will assist stations and producers who aim for the best in broadcasting good music, in broadcasting exciting plays, and in broadcasting reports on the whole fascinating range of human activity. It will try to prove that what educates can also be exciting. It will get part of its support from our Government. But it will be carefully guarded from Government or from party control. It will be free, and it will be independent—and it will belong to all of our people.

Television is still a young invention. But we have learned already that it has immense—even revolutionary—power to change, to change our lives. I hope that those who lead the Corporation will direct that power toward the great and not the trivial purposes. At its best, public television would help make our Nation a replica of the old Greek marketplace, where public affairs took place in view of all the citizens.

What hath man wrought? And how will man use his miracles? The answer just begins with public broadcasting.

In 1862, the Morrill Act set aside lands in every State—lands which belonged to the people—and it set them aside in order to build the land-grant colleges of the Nation.

So today we rededicate a part of the airwaves—which belong to all the people—and we dedicate them for the enlightenment of all the people. I believe the time has come to stake another claim in the name of all the people, stake a claim based upon the combined resources of communications. I believe the time has come to enlist the computer and the satellite, as well as television and radio, and to enlist them in the cause of education.

If we are up to the obligations of the next century and if we are to be proud of the next century as we are of the past two centuries, we have got to quit talking so much about what has happened in the past two centuries and start talking about what is going to happen in the next century beginning in 1976.

So I think we must consider new ways to build a great network for knowledge—not just a broadcast system, but one that employs every means of sending and storing information that the individual can use.

Think of the lives that this would change: the student in a small college could tap the resources of a great university.

Yes, the student in a small college tapping the resources of the greatest university in the hemisphere.

> • *The country doctor getting help from a distant laboratory or a teaching hospital;*
> • *a scholar in Atlanta might draw instantly on a library in New York;*
> • *a famous teacher could reach with ideas and inspirations into some far-off classroom, so that no child need be neglected.*

Eventually, I think this electronic knowledge bank could be as valuable as the Federal Reserve Bank.

And such a system could involve other nations, too—it could involve them in a partnership to share knowledge and to thus enrich all mankind.

A wild and visionary idea? Not at all. Yesterday's strangest dreams are today's headlines and change is getting swifter every moment.

I have already asked my advisers to begin to explore the possibility of a network for knowledge—and then to draw up a suggested blueprint for it.

In 1844, when Henry Thoreau heard about Mr. Morse's telegraph, he made his sour comment about the race for faster communication. "Perchance," he warned, "the first news which will leak through into the broad, flapping American ear will be that Princess Adelaide has the whooping cough."

We do have skeptic comments on occasions. But I don't want you to be that skeptic. I do believe that we have important things to say to one another—and we have the wisdom to match our technical genius.

In that spirit this morning, I have asked you to come here and be participants with me in this great movement for the next century, the Public Broadcasting Act of 1967.

C.

Characteristics of Harwood Innovation Spaces

Characteristics of a Harwood Innovation Space	What It Means	How to Get It
Space	*You must literally create space in the day for people to innovate.*	*Set aside a dedicated time*
Shared	*You must make learning a shared value and venture in the space.*	*Create a safe space with agreed upon ground rules and norms. Post them.*
Over Time	*You must hold the space open over time because innovation and learning take time.*	*Be highly vigilant about keeping the Innovation Space open over time.*
Intentional	*You must make learning and interacting a top priority and keep at it.*	*Continually draw lessons and ideas from the work—and its meaning for people and their work.*
Step Up	*You must hold one another accountable. People must genuinely engage to learn and innovate.*	*Discuss the group's performance from time to time.*

D.

Harwood Significance Barometer: Traits of Boundary-Spanning Organizations

Factor	We Want an Organization That...
Connects and Convenes	*Creates space for people who might not otherwise get together to work productively on community concerns.*
Candid Friend	*Is a candid friend who holds up a mirror to the community so people can see common or important challenges.*
Sticks with Community	*Demonstrates a commitment over time in work with the community; sets realistic objectives and follows through.*
Creates Understanding	*Helps inform people and build understanding on critical topics and issues to the community.*
Builds Community Resources	*Creates long-term capacity for change in the community.*
Innovates and Collaborates	*Creates new ideas and spins them off to other groups once they are up and running.*
Rooted in Community	*Starts with the community's aspirations and needs— putting the interests of the community front and center.*

OVERALL STATION RATING:

ACKNOWLEDGEMENTS

THERE ARE MANY PEOPLE to thank for the incredible work of the Community Engagement Initiative, and those whose worked helped make this book possible.

Through her visionary and innovative leadership, Patricia Harrison, CEO of the Corporation for Public Broadcasting made CEO a possibility. We wish to thank the staff of the 12 CEO stations. CEO was only possible because of the effort of people like Cheryl Head, Delinda Mworka, Mary Hanks, and others at CPB.

The Harwood Institute's project team worked tirelessly to coach and support the work of the stations. Our team included: David Moore, John Creighton, Melanie Kadlic Meren, Brad Rourke, Eric Rigaud, Cindy Page, Ann Hayward, and Christine Donohoo. Ryan Seashore helped coordinate design and publication.

Our editor was Harris Dienstfrey. We are grateful to him for his clear pen, flexibility and thoughtful suggestions. It is a far better book for his contributions.

We wish to thank John Dedrick, vice president and director of programs at the Kettering Foundation. His support led to the writing and production of this book.

We are indebted to David Mathews, the president of the Kettering Foundation. For 20 years he has partnered with the Harwood Institute and, in that time, his passionate and unswerving dedication to improving democracy in America and beyond has been a source of inspiration.

A postscript from Aaron:

I am deeply grateful to my parents, Richard Leavy and Christine Jones-Leavy, my sister Katie Leavy, and "brother" Mark Seide for their lifetime of support, guidance, and patience. Since NPR was the soundtrack to my childhood, the chance to work with, learn from, and document the power these stations have to create stronger communities has been a great joy. Lastly, I'd like to thank the mentors who seem to have found me when I needed them most: Tom Peet, Paul Dawson, Dan Cramer, Robert Richman, Tim Connolly, and Richard Harwood.

ABOUT
RICHARD HARWOOD

For more than 20 years, Richard C. Harwood has been dedicated to transforming our public and political lives by supporting individuals, organizations and communities in their quest to create change.

This passion for meaningful change and *making hope real* has led to the development of a practical, focused approach towards doing this work that has been proven effective.

His belief in the innate potential of people to come together to make a difference in the world led him to found The Harwood Institute for Public Innovation. Since its founding the Institute has partnered with some of the largest nonprofits in the world, as well as foundations and businesses to help people create meaningful change.

He is the author of *Make Hope Real* (2008) as well as *Hope Unraveled* (2005), and numerous articles, essays and op-eds. He is a commentator and contributor on national and syndicated television, newspapers, radio and web sites, including MSNBC, NPR, The Christian Science Monitor, CNN's Inside Politics, The New

Hour with Jim Lehrer, Special Report with Brit Hume, C-SPAN, and many other media outlets.

Rich is a teacher and speaker, inspiring hundreds of audiences, and making a strong case for his philosophy of *turning outward*, being relevant, choosing *intentionally*, and staying true to themselves and their urge to create change.

ABOUT
AARON LEAVY

Aaron Leavy serves as National Editorial Advisor for the Harwood Institute. In this position, he helps to develop, diffuse, and produce Harwood content and capture the stories of those using our work.

Prior to joining the Harwood Institute, Leavy worked as a research associate for Belden Russonello & Stewart, a national communications and research firm. He has also worked on campaigns in every Continental time zone, serving as assistant to the campaign manager for the 2002 Paul Wellstone campaign and the Iowa Director of Special Projects for Dean for America.

Leavy graduated from Oberlin College in 2001 with a BA in politics. He lives in the Mt. Pleasant neighborhood of Washington and is an avid back packer.

About the Harwood Institute for Public Innovation

If you turn outward and become more intentional in your choices and judgments in creating change you can have greater impact and relevance in your community.

The Harwood Institute for Public Innovation inspires and guides people to step forward and take action rooted in their community and stay true to themselves. We work with individuals, organizations, and communities to turn outward and develop their ability to make more intentional choices and judgments that lead to impact. After 20 years of innovating, we are taking our approach to scale to allow people to make these ideas their own. To achieve this goal we are partnering with organizations, such as United Way Worldwide, the Corporation for Public Broadcasting, and the w.k. Kellogg Foundation.

Founded by Richard C. Harwood in reaction to the cynicism and distrust that permeates much of politics and public life, the Harwood Institute is today a leading change organization, recognized nationally for a unique approach to breaking down barriers and empowering people to make progress in improving their communities.

Since its inception in 1989, the Harwood Institute has worked with communities, organizations, and individuals across the country—from Flint, Michigan; to Las Vegas, Nevada; and from Binghamton, New York; to San Francisco. Harwood principles have been successfully applied in the public, private, academic, and nonprofit sectors, including, public libraries and school systems, newspapers and public broadcasting, United Ways and other community-based organizations. Harwood helps these organizations and individuals turn outward and engage with their communities in new ways.

During years of hands-on innovation in communities across the country, the Harwood Institute created a set of field-tested tools and frameworks that have become the foundation of our approach and the basis for the practice that we help public innovators to develop for themselves. To learn more visit: **www.theharwoodinstitute.org**.

About the Kettering Foundation

Kettering Foundation is an operating and research foundation rooted in the American tradition of innovative research. The foundation does not make grants. Its founder, Charles F. Kettering, holder of more than 200 patents, was best known for his invention of the automobile self-starter. He was interested, above all, in seeking practical answers to "the problems behind the problems." Established in 1927, the foundation today continues in that tradition, but the objective of the research now is to learn how democracy can work better. Its major programs of research are designed to shed light on what is required for strengthening public life. More about the Kettering Foundation can be found at www.kettering.org.